"This is an engaging book of stories that will empower parents and teachers to help kids deal with challenges like peer pressure and bullying."

Rep. Jim Ramstad
United States Congress

"Youth are immersed in lots of hot issues—Who am I? How do I treat others? How do I behave? What should I do when friends are pulling me in two different directions? Here is a wonderful resource to help kids make ethical and thoughtful choices consistent with their own values, undergirded by an empathic understanding of how others are feeling. In a world riddled with toxic cultural norms and peer pressure, here is an opportunity to think, feel, reflect, and decide about issues that will, at some time, confront every young person. What an invaluable resource for all adults—parents, teachers, and mentors—who care about the development of kids."

Marilyn Sharpe
Director of Christian Parenting and Intergenerational Ministry at
The Youth & Family Institute

"Sandra McLeod Humphrey knows kids and what they have to deal with. This collection of stories has the ring of truth and the sound of reality. Whether you're a school-age student, a parent, or one who works with young people, you need to read this book."

Michael L. Sherer
Editor of *Metro Lutheran Newspaper*
Minneapolis, Minnesota

HOT ISSUES
COOL CHOICES

Published 2007 by Prometheus Books

Inquiries should be addressed to
Prometheus Books
59 John Glenn Drive
Amherst, New York 14228–2119
VOICE: 716–691–0133, ext. 210
FAX: 716–691–0137
WWW.PROMETHEUSBOOKS.COM

11 10 09 08   5 4 3 2

Library of Congress Cataloging-in-Publication Data

Humphrey, Sandra McLeod.
    Hot issues, cool choices : facing bullies, peer pressure, popularity, and put-downs / by Sandra McLeod Humphrey ; illustrated by Brian Strassburg. — 1st American pbk. ed.
        p. cm.
    Includes bibliographical references.
    ISBN 978–1–59102–569–6
    1. Children—Conduct of life—Juvenile literature. 2. Success in children—Juvenile literature. I. Title.

BJ1631.H84 2007
155.42'48—dc22

2007027082

Printed in the United States of America on acid-free paper

HOT ISSUES
COOL CHOICES

Facing Bullies, Peer Pressure, Popularity, and Put-Downs

SANDRA McLEOD HUMPHREY

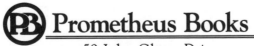

Prometheus Books

59 John Glenn Drive
Amherst, New York 14228-2119

In memory of Tommy

who took his own life
at the age of twelve years,
two months, and ten days

ACKNOWLEDGMENTS

I would like to thank the parents who told me their children's stories, the teachers who allowed me to talk to their students, and, most of all, the students who so willingly shared their sometimes very painful stories.

THE GOLDEN RULE

"Do to others as you would have them do to you."
(Luke 6:31 NIV)

CONTENTS

CONTENTS

AUTHOR'S NOTE

The **Golden Rule** is an old rule, but it's still a good rule to live by. My hope in writing this book is that it will help you to become a kinder, more compassionate human being and that you will treat others the way you want them to treat you.

Did you know that there are kids out there who don't even want to get out of bed in the morning because they know what going to school means for them?

It can mean being teased and taunted by other kids.

It can mean being excluded and rejected by other kids.

It can mean being afraid that you're going to be physically assaulted and possibly hurt.

And, unfortunately, sometimes it can even mean that you just can't hang in there any longer, so you give up and take your own life.

If you *are* one of the cool kids at your school, this book is for you.

And if you're *not* one of the cool kids at your school, this book is especially for you.

Emerson Elementary isn't a real school, but it could be any elementary school anywhere. And the students at Emerson aren't real kids, but the problems they're facing are real problems, and the choices they're making are real choices.

So come along and join the students at Emerson Elementary and help them make some cool choices!

ANGELINA AND ME

My name is Erica, and my life is like totally wrecked! Maybe Angelina didn't mean to wreck it, and then again maybe she did.

You won't understand unless I start at the beginning. Don't worry, I don't mean the very beginning.

We're just going to rewind to last month when my cousin Angelina came to stay with us for a few weeks while her parents worked out a few problems.

Now I've got to tell you right up front that Angelina and I have nothing in common. We never have had anything in common, and we never will have anything in common.

She likes volleyball, French, and pepperoni pizza. Me, I like swimming, science, and spaghetti with lots of garlic.

And we don't even look anything alike either. No one would ever know we're related. She's tall and skinny with long blond hair and blue eyes. Me, I'm what my dad calls "pleasingly plump" with short dark hair and brown eyes.

And that's not the worst of it. Our personalities are like totally polar opposites. I'm shy and more comfortable with books than people while Angelina attracts people like fly-paper.

My dad tells everyone that Angelina could sell snowshoes to a penguin. Me, I think Angelina just loves to hear herself talk.

I think Angelina is what some people might call a "free spirit" because she just does whatever she feels like doing whenever she feels like doing it, without even thinking first.

Like last week we were rollerblading around the lake, and she sees this little old woman in a long black coat all hunched over digging through one of the dumpsters. Good grief, I was sweating buckets, and the woman was wearing this really raggedy old black coat down to her ankles.

I figured the woman was probably what people call a "bag lady" because it looked like she had all her worldly possessions stuffed into the huge brown paper bag next to her.

I'd read about people like her in books and I'd even seen a few on the TV news, but I had never seen one up close in real life like this before.

Well, anyway, I was just going to keep on rollerblading, minding my own business, but what does Angelina do? She stops dead in her tracks and rummages through her backpack till she finds her bag lunch.

You're not going to believe this, but then she gives her lunch to the bag lady. Just like that, she gives the woman her whole lunch.

It was just a cheese sandwich and an apple, but it meant that now I had to share my lunch with Angelina. That's what I mean about Angelina doing crazy stuff without even thinking about the consequences before she does them.

So, anyway, while I'm busy moaning and groaning to myself about having to share my lunch with Angelina, that bag lady just plants this big old kiss right there on Angelina's cheek.

I couldn't believe my eyes! It was just a cheese sandwich and an apple, but you'd think Angelina had just given her a bag full of diamonds.

Since I was beginning to feel kind of embarrassed for all of us, I skated over to the water fountain and pretended to be taking a drink.

I told myself that I wasn't going to ask Angelina any questions. Not even one. I was just going to pretend that I hadn't seen anything at all. But when Angelina caught up to me, the words just popped right out of my mouth before I could stop them.

"So why did you do it? Why did you give that woman your lunch?"

"Because she looked hungry."

That's right, that's all Angelina said. Then she just skated off like there was nothing even a teensy bit unusual about giving her whole lunch away to a total stranger!

So, anyway, now you see what I mean about Angelina. I'm stuck with her for two more weeks, and who knows what crazy thing she's going to do next! I think maybe I should talk to her and tell her to get her act together.

What do you think I should do?

MORE TO THINK ABOUT:

- What do you think Erica should do? Why?
- Why do you think Angelina gave her lunch to the bag lady?
- How do you think she felt after she did it?
- Do you think you're more like Erica or Angelina? Why?

TRADING PLACES:

- If you were a bag lady, how would you like to be treated, and how would you feel if someone did what Angelina did?

ME, MYSELF, AND I

My name is Dylan, but sometimes I think I should have three different names to go with my three personalities.

First, I guess I'd better tell you a little about our school. We have three different groups at our school: the smart kids, the average kids, and the popular kids.

During lunch the smart kids sit with the smart kids. The average kids sit with the average kids. And the popular kids sit with the other popular kids.

I don't think people should be stuck in categories, but at our school they are. That's just the way it is, and that's probably the way it will always be.

My friend Matthew belongs to the popular group, and for a while I actually hung out with the popular kids. But it just didn't feel right. I wasn't interested in the same things they were interested in.

They were way more into sports than I was, and I cared more about good grades than they did. So I pretended to care more about sports than I really did, and I pretended not to care about my grades as much.

Some of the kids in that group spent the whole week talking

about whose parties they were going to and which kids were going to be there.

I could care less about parties but I wanted to fit in, so I talked about parties, too. On Monday I talked about the parties I had been to over the weekend, and on Friday I talked about the parties I was going to go to.

I've got to tell you, this was *not* the real me doing the talking. I was just saying whatever I could to fit in.

But I hung out with those guys anyway because, at the time, I thought that was the cool thing to do. And Matthew was my best friend, so I wanted to belong to his group.

For a while I even hung out with the smart kids, but I didn't really fit in with that group either. Those kids were REALLY smart!

They were all taking "challenge classes" and they spent most of their time reading books and working on independent study projects.

My friend Ricardo is the class "brainiac" and he belongs to this group. He's never had less than an A on anything in his entire life.

I'm pretty smart, but I'm not *that* smart. I don't even play chess with him anymore because he usually beats me in six moves. Or less.

I never felt like I fit in with those kids either. I always felt like I was being tested and could never really measure up to those guys.

That's why sometimes I think I'm developing a split personality. I have to act one way when I hang out with Matthew and his group, and I have to act a totally different way when I hang out with Ricardo and his group.

It seems I have to change my personality to fit in with either Matthew's group or Ricardo's group. I don't think I'm being the real me when I'm with either group.

So then I decided to hang out with the guys in the average group, but I didn't really fit in any better with them.

The truth is that I'm a little bit like all three groups, but I'm not 100 percent like any one group.

I like to go fishing with Antonio from the average group. I like going to football games with Matthew from the popular group. And I like studying for my social studies tests with Ricardo from the smart group.

I think what this means is that I don't really fit into any of the three groups, which leaves me with *no* group. I'm kind of like the man without a country, only in my case, I'm the kid without a group.

Right now Matthew is pressuring me to be part of his group. Ricardo is telling me that I'll be sorry if I don't stick with his group. And, if I drop out of Antonio's group, I might just end up losing my best fishing buddy.

What do you think I should do?

MORE TO THINK ABOUT:

- What do you think Dylan should do? Why?
- Do you belong to a group or clique?
- Do you think it's OK not to belong to any particular group? Why or why not?
- Why do you think kids divide up into groups or cliques?

TRADING PLACES:

- Have you ever felt like Dylan?

MUSICAL CHAIRS

I feel like I'm on a popularity treadmill and can't get off!

Hi, my name is Nikki, and ever since first grade I've wanted to belong to Caitlin's group. The popular group.

Then this year in fifth grade my dream came true. I was suddenly in Caitlin's group, and for the first time in my life, I was one of the "popular" girls.

But now that I'm in Caitlin's group, I'm more confused than ever. It's like the rules change every day. One day I'm Caitlin's best friend, and the next day, it's like I'm invisible and no one in the group even speaks to me.

Today I'm invisible. Again. I'm sitting at Caitlin's table in the lunchroom, but everyone's pretty much ignoring me. My stomach feels like it's got lead marbles sitting in it.

I'm staring at Caitlin's purple nails. A purple I'd never have the nerve to wear in a hundred years. Make that a gazillion years.

Right now Caitlin is giving Taylor a hard time because Taylor didn't wear her hair the way she was supposed to today. She was supposed to wear it down with no hair band, but she's got it tied up in a pony tail with a red ribbon.

That's something I've learned about Caitlin's group. There

are rules about everything. Rules about what we wear, how we do our hair, who we can hang out with, and especially who we can and cannot sit with at lunch. Caitlin has more rules than my mom does.

Taylor reminds me of a turtle trying to pull its head into its shell. She's just sitting there real quiet, looking paler and paler while I watch the happy expression slide right off her face.

I know just how Taylor feels because last week Caitlin was on my case because I sat with Sumaya at lunch while we worked on our social studies project.

Caitlin warned me that I would be out of her group if that ever happened again.

Sometimes I feel like a Ping-Pong ball bouncing back and forth across the net, not wanting to stop on either side. But I know that eventually I'll have to land somewhere. And to be honest, I'm not always sure on which side I want to stop.

Ever since I joined Caitlin's group, I've felt like I'm on a roller coaster. One day I feel like I'm on top of the world, and the next day I'm in the pits.

You do one little thing wrong and you're like on probation while Caitlin and her group decide whether you're still "in" or whether you're "out."

I thought it was stressful trying to get *into* her group, but I think it's more stressful just trying to *stay* in her group.

Being in Caitlin's group is like being stuck in quicksand. Each step I take, the deeper I sink, and at the rate I'm going, it won't be long until I'm completely swallowed up. I will end up being Caitlin's clone just like everyone else in her group.

Caitlin and Cheryl exchange a look I can't read, and then Caitlin says to Taylor, "Maybe you should sit at one of the other tables. We don't really have room for you at our table today."

I watch the blood totally drain from Taylor's face. The whole lunchroom gets so quiet, you could hear a popsicle melt.

Taylor doesn't say a word. She just gets up from the table and takes her tray to a table in the corner. She sits down there all by herself with her back to us.

Then Caitlin picks up a slab of pizza and smiles this little smile that isn't really a smile at all. I feel my lunch moving back up my throat, and the marbles in my stomach have now turned to bricks.

I just sit there for a minute, my cheeks on fire. I can't believe this is really happening. I'm sure everyone in the whole lunchroom is staring at us. I can feel their laser eyes burning into my back.

If I leave the table, I know I'll be out of Caitlin's group for good. But can I leave Taylor feeling totally humiliated and sitting all by herself like that?

I know what I want to do. I want to leave my table and move to Taylor's table. But do I have the courage to do it?

What do you think I should do?

MORE TO THINK ABOUT:

- What do you think Nikki should do? Why?
- How do you feel about Caitlin?
- How do you feel about Caitlin's group?
- Would you want to be in her group? Why or why not?

TRADING PLACES:

- How do you think Taylor feels?

NO, NO,
A THOUSAND TIMES NO!

My name is Eric, and my life is about to self-destruct right before my eyes. And this time it's not even my fault!

You won't understand my problem unless I tell you about Jeremy because *he's* my problem.

Jeremy is new this year and I've got to tell you, this kid is different. And I do mean D-I-F-F-E-R-E-N-T!

While my friends and I are talking football scores, Jeremy is spouting off about all the damage we're doing to the ozone layer and how fossil fuels can cause global warming.

And after school while the rest of us guys are running up and down the soccer field getting ready for soccer practice, Jeremy is out there picking up litter.

Right now he's picking up empty pop cans and tossing them in the recycling bin. It's like he thinks he's on his own personal mission to save the Earth.

I know, I know. I still haven't told you my problem. So listen up because I'm going to do that right now.

Every year I have a Halloween party and invite all my friends. My mom bakes the best brownies on Planet Earth, and my dad whips up his special apple cider.

We all wear costumes, and even my parents dress up. Last

year my mom wore this cool kangaroo costume, and my dad dressed up like a pirate.

Well, anyway, back to my problem. My friends and I are out there by the soccer field waiting for Coach Williams and making our last-minute plans for my party while Jeremy is out there doing what he's always doing. Picking up pop cans.

I guess he must have heard us talking because he comes up to me and asks me right out if he can come to my party. Just like that, he asks me if he can come to my party. That is just so totally uncool.

Now there is no way I'm going to invite Jeremy to my party. But I can't come right out and tell him that he can't come because he is a total geek! So what do I say?

I look over at Tyler for some help here. But he's busy staring at his feet, so it looks like I'm on my own.

Just then Coach Williams blows his whistle, and I'm saved by the bell. Or, in this case, the whistle. I tell Jeremy I'll talk to him later, and I jog off onto the soccer field with the rest of the guys.

While Coach Williams is busy calling out all the plays for our next game, I'm busy running my own plays through my head. The only thing I know for sure is that there's no way I'm going to invite Jeremy to my party or everyone will think I'm as weird as he is. What I need is a plan.

Like maybe I can tell him our house is too small to invite any more kids. Nah! That sounds pretty lame even to me.

Or maybe I can tell him that it's too late to invite any more kids because my mom has already bought all the party stuff. Nah! Even a total dork wouldn't believe that.

I need time to do some serious thinking. Time to come up with an excuse which won't totally blow him away but will save my party.

As I'm running up and down the soccer field, so many ideas are spinning around through my head that I'm beginning to get a monster headache.

I'm just hoping that practice will last long enough for me to come up with something. Something that even Jeremy will believe. I don't want to annihilate the kid or anything, but there's just no way I can invite him to my party.

Soccer practice is winding down, and I still haven't come up with any decent ideas to save my party. My only hope is that Jeremy has finished picking up his pop cans and gone home. Then I'll have all night to come up with a plan.

As I come off the field, I kind of half close my eyes hoping that I won't see Jeremy. But there he is, big as life, waiting for me.

It's not like I have a zillion friends or anything, but I just know that if I invite Jeremy to my party, I'll lose the few friends I do have.

What do you think I should do?

MORE TO THINK ABOUT:

- What do you think Eric should do? Why?
- How do you feel about Jeremy?
- Do you think Eric will really lose all his friends if he invites Jeremy to his party?
- Do you think Jeremy knows how Eric and his friends feel about him?

TRADING PLACES:

- How would you feel if you were Jeremy and you weren't invited to Eric's party?

BIRTHDAY BLUES

Hi, my name is Molly and I've got some great news! That is, I *had* some great news.

My birthday is next month, so I invited Tara and Chelsea over to help me write the party invitations. Tara and Chelsea have been my best friends for just about forever.

I show them my invitation list, which includes all the girls in our class, and give them some cards to address.

But one look at my party list and Tara just about goes into orbit.

"You're not going to invite 'Blimpo,' are you?" Tara sputters, dramatically puffing out her cheeks and wrinkling up her nose. "Remember when she came to the school dance in that yellow dress with the ruffles? It was like King Kong pretending to be Cinderella."

I know who she means, of course. She means Anna. I've got to admit Anna is pretty heavy, and I don't think she has very many friends.

But she has a great sense of humor, and I loved being in our class play with her last year. She can do really cool imitations of famous people, and it's fun to hang out with her.

I'm going to tell my friends that I want to keep Anna on my list, but before I can say anything, it's Chelsea's turn to go ballistic.

"Why is Casey on the list? She's weird, and she wouldn't fit in. You just *can't* invite her!"

Casey does have dyslexia, but she's just as smart as anyone else in our class. And she's a lot smarter than me in math. Besides, I really like her a lot.

I watch while Tara draws heavy red lines through Anna's name and Casey's name.

Meanwhile Chelsea is reviewing the rest of the names on my list and wincing in pain. She's holding her stomach like she's getting ready to barf.

"Good grief, Molly, you can't invite Louisa. She's always got her head stuck in a book and never talks to anyone. No one ever invites her to any of their parties because she's so shy. She probably wouldn't come anyway even if you did invite her."

Tara shakes her head and gives Chelsea a thumbs-up. "Chelsea's right. We just want to invite girls who are fun. Girls who are popular. So that means no invites for Sumaya or Tamika either. I don't think they even know how to bowl, and they wouldn't have any fun just watching the rest of us."

As Chelsea and Tara sit there reviewing my list and crossing off names, my good mood is suddenly doing a U-turn. Something I had looked forward to doing with my two best friends is turning into a monumental disaster.

My party list is getting shorter by the minute. Pretty soon there won't be anyone left on the list but the three of us. I'm beginning to wonder if I should even have a party this year.

Then Tara holds up my list and points to Melissa's name. She rolls her eyes dramatically the way she always does when she's trying to make a point.

"I can't believe you're even thinking of inviting Melissa. Melissa with the Coke-bottle glasses and the stringy hair. Remember last week when she wore that bright neon green sweat suit with matching socks? Just looking at her gave me a headache."

I shrug my no-big-deal shrug and tell myself this isn't a matter of life or death. But still I feel a lump forming in my throat and a huge rock sitting in the pit of my stomach.

It's *my* party. I should invite whoever I want to invite. But do I really want to get into a big hassle with my two best friends?

I feel like I'm being pulled in two different directions, and I can feel my stomach twisting into a knot. Do I keep quiet and go along with Tara and Chelsea? Or do I do what I really want to do and invite all the girls in my class?

Both Tara and Chelsea have their eyes glued on me waiting for me to say something, but I don't know what to do.

What do you think I should do?

MORE TO THINK ABOUT:

- What do you think Molly should do? Why?
- What do you think of Molly's party list?
- If you were Molly, what would you tell Tara and Chelsea?
- How do you decide which kids to invite to your parties?

TRADING PLACES:

- If Molly doesn't invite all the girls in her class, how do you think those girls who aren't invited are going to feel?

HOT DOGS
AND OTHER DOGS

"I can't believe you did that. That is so gross!"

My name is Nick, and I'm staring at my best friend Radar who has just stuffed the rest of his hot dog into his mouth.

I cross my eyes and hold my nose. "Who ever heard of peanut butter and jelly on a hot dog? You're lucky you didn't throw up all over the table."

Radar shoves the empty mustard jar across the table toward me and shoots me another grin. "You were out of mustard, so I had to improvise. A little catsup, a little mayo, and a lot of peanut butter and jelly. Don't knock it till you've tried it."

I watch him wipe his mouth with his sleeve while I try to keep from barfing myself.

Then he lets loose with another huge grin. "I had to make it interesting, didn't I?"

That just about sums up my relationship with Radar. Being with him is never dull. He's very smart, but I think he's also a little strange.

His real name is William Emerson Stevens, but I call him Radar because he can see an ant crawling across a carpet from

twenty feet away and he can hear our refrigerator door open from his house next door. Well, maybe he doesn't really hear the refrigerator door open, but he does seem to show up whenever we're sitting down to eat.

He can also make his eyeballs roll all the way up in his head, so you can't see anything but the whites. He does this whenever he's trying to make a point.

Suddenly I feel a sharp jab in my ribs. "So what do you think? Should we do it or not?"

I have no clue what he's talking about, so I just grin back at him. "I don't know. What do *you* want to do?"

"Nicholas, sometimes you are such a pain. You weren't even listening, were you?"

When Radar calls me "Nicholas," I know he's really upset. I shake my head and try to look properly sorry. "I guess not. I was just wishing we had something fun to do."

Now he is staring at me like I'm some strange specimen under a microscope, and he is no longer grinning.

"Earth-to-Nicholas. Are you listening now? That's just exactly what I was talking about before you zoned out on me. So do you want to help out at the County Animal Shelter or not?"

Now it all started to come back to me. How Ms. Wilson, our school guidance counselor, had talked about organizing a group to help out at the local animal shelter every Wednesday afternoon after school.

At the time it had sounded like fun, but now I wasn't so sure. Did I really want to give up one afternoon every week? Only five kids had signed up so far.

I stopped glopping peanut butter on my bread and stared back at him. "I'm not so sure I want to do it after all. The only kids who have signed up are kids we don't even hang out with. None of the popular kids have signed up."

Radar gave me his best I-could-care-less shrug and groaned. "So who cares who's signed up? I know that I want to do it! Do you want to do it with me or not?"

I zapped him with *the look*. The look that says I know something he doesn't know. He hates that look!

"So just this," I said, shifting into my best know-it-all mode. "If we work at the animal shelter with kids like Louisa and Connor, we'll end up on the 'loser' list just like them."

There's a huge slice of silence, and I can tell that Radar's doing some serious thinking. I know that he knows I'm right, even if he doesn't want to come right out and admit it.

Then he says, "So what's wrong with Louisa and Connor anyway? Since when are they on what you call 'the loser' list?"

Sometimes Radar is like this. He likes to argue a point even when he knows I'm right. He's always talking about being an attorney some day, and I think he just likes to practice his arguments on me.

I know that Radar knows what I'm saying is true, and I know that he's going to end up not going to the animal shelter.

What do you think Radar should do?

MORE TO THINK ABOUT:

- How do you feel about Radar?
- How do you feel about Nicholas?
- Do you think you're more like Nicholas or Radar? Why?
- Do you think Louisa and Connor are really "losers"?

TRADING PLACES:

- If you were Radar, what would you do? Why?

FROSTED CUPCAKES AND NO-NAME JEANS

Hi, my name is Rachel, and I'm holding in my hand an invitation that could change my entire life! An invitation to join KK's secret club.

"KK" stands for Kristina Kallan, and her club really isn't a secret because everyone knows who's in it. Only seven of the most popular girls in school!

They eat lunch at the same table every day in the school lunchroom, they wear identical purple sweaters on Fridays, and they're always invited to the coolest parties.

The kids call them "KK's Girls" and everyone I know would give a million bucks to belong to KK's club.

Correction: Make that *almost* everyone. Everyone except my best friend Marissa who just does her own thing and could care less about what anyone else is doing.

While everyone else is wearing Reeboks and Adidas, she's wearing athletic shoes she found on a table at a flea market.

She doesn't even own a pair of designer jeans. She says that kids only wear labels to impress other kids and that she'd rather spend the extra money on a good book.

I think most people would consider Marissa definitely uncool. And to be honest, before I got the invitation to join KK's club, I wasn't all that cool myself.

Thoughts of Marissa fade as I squeeze my invitation into my backpack and begin counting the minutes till noon.

I still can't believe I will actually be sitting at KK's table. It's like being invited to lunch at the White House. Only better!

In math class while Ms. Jackson drones on about percentages and probabilities, I'm busy calculating my own probabilities.

Without being a member of KK's club, the probability of my ever being anybody is zip, zero, zilch. Belonging to KK's club will mean that I will no longer be a nobody. I will now be *somebody*.

By the time the lunch bell rings and I walk into the lunchroom, I feel like I've walked through Alice's Looking Glass and come out the other side.

The KK girls are already at their table. When they see me, KK waves and flashes me one of her dazzling smiles. Even her teeth seem to glitter.

I can feel some of the kids at the other tables staring at me. I know they're probably wondering how I, a former geek, managed to get accepted into the most exclusive club in school.

To be honest, I've been wondering the same thing. And a few minutes later I find out.

KK is wearing pink jeans, a pink sweater, and a pink ribbon around her blond ponytail. She looks like a walking clump of cotton candy. Or maybe a pink-frosted cupcake.

But it's Lori who does most of the talking, her voice as soft as melted butter.

"You know, Rachel, we've been wanting to talk to you for a long time now. We all think it's just so cool the way you can type up all your book reports and science projects in no time at all. It takes me forever just to type one little paragraph."

Then Natalie chimes in. "Lori's right. No one can type as fast as you and no one is as good a speller."

I can feel my stomach knotting up and all my senses going on a red alert, but I do my best to keep a smile pasted on my face while I wait for Lori to get to the point.

"Since all this writing stuff is so easy for you, we were thinking that if you were part of our group, then you could help us with all our papers. You know, kind of edit the rough drafts for us, correct the spelling, and then type them up."

The knot in my stomach is growing as Natalie chimes back in. "It would be kind of like pooling our talents where everybody wins. You help us, we help you. We'll see that you get invited to all the cool parties."

My smile is quickly dimming to total blackout as their words begin to sink in, and my brain is spinning as images of frosted cupcakes and no-name jeans begin whirling around through my head.

What do you think I should do?

MORE TO THINK ABOUT:

- What do you think Rachel should do? Why?
- Why do you think Rachel wants to join KK's group so badly?
- How do you feel about Marissa?
- How do you feel about KK and her friends?

TRADING PLACES:

- If you were in Rachel's place, would you join KK's group? Why or why not?

TESTING, TESTING . . .

My name is Peter and I'm beginning to think the guys are right when they call me a loser.

My problem started way back in second grade when I got treated for lice. After that, all the other kids called me the "diseased boy" and never let me touch them. They wouldn't let me touch their things either because they didn't want my "disease germs."

They even made up a game they called "Poison Ivy." I was always "it" and whenever I got close to tagging anyone, they would yell "Poison Ivy" and run like crazy.

I guess the name stuck because every time we were on the playground during recess, kids would point at me and shout "Poison Ivy!" Then they'd run, and I'd be left standing there all by myself.

Second grade was the pits. The absolute pits. But third grade wasn't much better. That's when Nigel invited everyone in our class to his birthday party except Connor and me.

I'll never know why he didn't invite us, but he didn't. I don't know how Connor felt, but I know how I felt. I felt like somehow I had messed up again, and it was all my fault. That I was a loser!

I never told my parents about the party, so they never knew how bad I felt. I figured it was *my* problem, and I didn't want them to worry about having a loser kid.

Then last year in fourth grade I got braces on my teeth, and Tyrone was forever making jokes about them. I was used to him calling me "metal-mouth" and "zipper-lips," but then he started calling me "mush-mouth" and imitating what he called my "lispth."

I think November 15 will be burned into my memory bank forever. That was the day that I almost blew!

We were in the school lunchroom and I was sitting by myself as usual. Tyrone was two tables away, but I could still hear him sounding off about my braces and imitating my "lispth."

I knew I was losing my cool as my face burned and imaginary steam shot out of my ears. I really wanted to go over to Tyrone's table and dump his whole lunch tray right on his head.

But I knew exactly where that would get me. Nowhere! Tyrone and his friends would have me right where they wanted me. I'd be the one to get in trouble, and they would just act all innocent like they didn't know why I was so upset.

I didn't know what to do, so I didn't do anything. I just left the lunchroom and hung out on the playground until my next class.

I guess kids see me as an easy target because I just go into my little shell and don't ever fight back. But where would fighting back get me? It's them against me, and we all know who would come out the winners and who would come out the loser.

Sometimes it feels like I'm being tested to see how much I can take before I break.

The only kid who has it worse is this kid from Bolivia. His name is Tony and he speaks with an accent, so Tyrone goes around imitating Tony's accent the same way he imitates my "lispth."

Tony's also really skinny and not very good in sports, so he gets teased about that, too. Tyrone and his friends call him "Bony Tony" and give him a hard time whenever they can.

Like in gym class yesterday. Tony was up to bat and Tyrone yells that he's going to miss the ball, so of course, he *does* miss the ball. Then Tyrone yells at him because he missed the ball.

I don't know why Tyrone and his friends do the rotten things they do. Maybe it makes them feel tough. Maybe it's a power thing. I just don't know.

All I know is that they're making my life miserable. And I'm pretty sure Tony's life isn't too great either.

Ms. Wilson, our guidance counselor, is starting a group for kids who want to talk about any problems they're having at school. I'm seriously thinking of signing up.

I'm even thinking I might talk to Tony and see if he wants to sign up, too. Or maybe he'll think I'm butting into his business and just wants to be left alone.

What do you think I should do?

MORE TO THINK ABOUT:

- What do you think Peter should do? Why?
- Why do you think Tyrone and his friends bully Peter and Tony?
- How do you feel about Tyrone and his friends?
- If you were Peter, would you join Ms. Wilson's group? Why or why not?

TRADING PLACES:

- If you were Peter or Tony, how would you feel?

PROMISES, PROMISES

I hung up the phone and just sat there counting the loops in the phone cord. I was still counting loops five minutes later when the phone rang again.

My name is Erin, and that was my best friend, Kendall, on the phone. She was calling back to say she couldn't go bowling on Saturday after all.

I knew exactly what that meant. It meant that in the last five minutes Kendall had gotten a better offer. Five minutes ago, bowling had sounded good, but now something else sounded a lot better.

Kendall and I have been best friends since first grade. But the Kendall I know now isn't the same Kendall I've known for the last four years.

I could always count on the old Kendall. If she said she was going to do something, I knew she would do it. If we made plans to see a movie or go skating, I knew I could count on her to do it.

But then last year she started hanging out with some of the popular kids, and now she cancels out on me any time she feels like it if she gets a better offer.

Like last summer. She was going to spend a week with my mom and me at our family cabin up north.

That is until Natasha invited her to go to Disney World for a week. The same week she was going to spend at our cabin. She told me that she was *really* sorry, but she knew I would understand. After all, how could anyone pass up a week at Disney World!

And then there was last month when she was going to go to my brother's soccer playoffs with us. Then she got invited to Matthew's surprise birthday party. I guess I don't have to tell you where she went!

Kendall and I met over her ninety-six pack of Crayolas back in first grade. I had forgotten to bring mine, and she shared hers with me.

After that, it seemed we did everything together. We took swimming lessons together. We took dance lessons together. We even got braces on our teeth at the same time.

I still have the BFF necklace she gave me in third grade, and I really thought we *would* be best friends forever. But then sometime between fourth and fifth grade, Kendall changed.

She began eating lunch with the popular girls whenever she could. And when there wasn't room at their table for her, then she ate lunch with me.

It's like she had first-choice friends and second-choice friends, and I was no longer her first choice.

Last week I decided to try talking to her. We were in my bedroom studying for a math test, and I tried telling her how I felt.

Well, that was a total catastrophe! The more I tried to tell her how I felt, the more she just denied everything.

I was beginning to feel like a bottle of soda that had been shaken up and was ready to explode. But it was Kendall who finally exploded. Her face turned as red as her hair, and she shot me down with all her guns blazing away.

At first she told me that I was imagining everything and that nothing had changed. But the more wound up she got, the more she began freaking out. That's when she began listing all the things she didn't like about me.

She ended up telling me that *I* was the one who had changed

bumping into me in the halls. He's even made me get down on my hands and knees so that he can sit on my back like a bench.

Everyone is terrified of Larry, which means that if Larry chooses you for a target, then you end up being everybody's target. Everyone wants to be Larry's friend just so they don't end up getting bullied. Whatever Larry wants, Larry gets.

So, anyway, that's why I was so glad to see Evan. I figured now he'd get all the teasing that I used to get. Like I said, Evan is even shorter than me and he's skinny as a skeleton.

It turned out I was 100 percent right. Larry and the other guys let up on me and began giving Evan a hard time instead. They call him "chicken" and go around saying, "Bok bok bok bok!" while they wave their arms up and down.

I think they like to tease him because it's so easy to make Evan mad. His ears get bright red and he like totally explodes every time.

I've told Evan to ignore the teasing because if he doesn't react, then it's no fun for the bullies. But I guess he can't help himself because he still explodes every single time. Sometimes he gets so upset that I think he might just burst into tears right there in front of everybody.

I've got to admit that I've even teased Evan a few times myself just to be accepted by the other guys. I guess for once in my life I wanted to see how it felt to be one of the bullies instead of the bully target.

To be honest, it didn't feel very good. I ended up feeling guilty because I know how it feels to be bullied and here I was doing the same thing to Evan.

Compared to some kids, I guess Evan and I don't have it so bad. I heard about a kid at Wilson Elementary who got tossed in the dumpster. By the time he managed to climb out, he was covered with so much gunk that he had to go straight home. I guess some of the plastic bags broke and he ended up sitting in a mess of spaghetti with spaghetti sauce all over him.

I also heard about some jocks at Wilson who hung a kid by his belt loops from a coat hook in the locker room and just left him there.

And my cousin knows a kid who hides behind his school

building every day after school because he's afraid to walk home by himself. There's a bully at the kid's school who trips him in the hallway, shoves him around on the playground, and threatens to beat him up. I guess that poor kid is trying to change schools.

Now I'm hanging out with some of the guys who used to bully me, but I don't really have any close friends because I don't trust anyone all that much anymore.

I don't know why some kids bully other kids, but I guess if you make someone else feel smaller, then maybe you feel bigger.

Right now the other guys are letting me hang out with them because Evan is the target. I don't really want to bully Evan, but the other guys won't let me hang out with them if I don't.

What do you think I should do?

MORE TO THINK ABOUT:

- What do you think Nathan should do? Why?
- How do you think bullies choose a "target"?
- Why do you think bullies "bully"?
- Why do you think Nathan bullied Evan when he knows how it feels to be bullied?

TRADING PLACES:

- Have you ever felt like Nathan or Evan?

FOLLOW THE LEADER

My name is Casey, and I'm dyslexic. For a long time, I thought I wasn't very smart. It seemed everyone learned to read and write so much faster than I did.

And it wasn't only the reading and writing. Sometimes I even had trouble finding the right words. I knew what I wanted to say, but the words just didn't seem to come out. It's like they were there, but I couldn't find them.

For a while my parents and teachers thought I just wasn't trying, but I *was* trying. That's when I got tested, and we found out I had a reading disorder called dyslexia.

Having dyslexia means that I have a problem with words. I have trouble recognizing and remembering words, and sometimes I even read words and letters backwards. Like sometimes I confuse a "d" for a "b."

It felt good to know I wasn't dumb after all, but finding a name for my problem really didn't help all that much.

There's this girl in my class who's been giving me a really hard time. Her name is Heather, and she's told just about everybody in the world how dumb I am.

She and her friends have even written stuff like "CASEY IS DUMB, DUMB, DUMB!" on the walls in the girls' bathroom.

And last week they wrote "DUMB, DUMBER, DUMBEST!" on my locker door with a bright red permanent marker.

There are some mornings I don't even want to get out of bed because I know what's waiting for me at school. Heather and her friends.

My problem with Heather began back in the third grade.

We were both stretched out on the floor next to each other painting scenery for our class play.

I was painting a tree, and I accidentally spilled the can of brown paint. The brown paint ran all over the yellow sunflower Heather was painting. For a minute she didn't say anything. She just sat back on her heels and stared at her sunflower.

Then the next thing I knew, she was on her feet standing over me and yelling at me at the top of her lungs. She called me every name she could think of, including "DUMB" and "STUPID."

I felt bad about wrecking her sunflower, but I didn't really think it was that big a deal. She could always just paint another sunflower. But it turned out that it *was* a very big deal to Heather.

After that, she just seemed to look for ways to bug me. It was like her mission in life was to make my life miserable.

Fourth grade was a little better because she began spending more time with her friends and had less time to pick on me. For a while I even thought she had forgotten about me.

But this year she's making fifth grade totally impossible for me. She's not only calling me names, but now she's started a rumor that I'm anorexic. And she's got all her friends spreading the rumor.

I am thin, but I've always been thin, and she knows that. Heather's the one who's always on some kind of diet while I'm always eating everything in sight, trying to gain a few pounds.

I'm pretty sure just about everyone in the entire school has heard the rumor because I see kids staring at me like they're trying to decide whether or not the rumor is true.

I feel like I should be wearing a neon sign that reads:

I AM NOT DUMB AND I AM NOT ANOREXIC!

I've tried everything. I've tried talking to Heather and telling her how I feel, but all she says is, "It's no big deal, can't you take a joke?"

Mostly I've tried ignoring her, but it's hard to ignore her when she and her friends are in my face spreading rumors and writing graffiti all over the place.

I haven't tried talking to Ms. Wilson, our guidance counselor, but what could she do? If she talks to Heather, that might just make things even worse. Then Heather will just tell everyone that I'm a snitch and can't even take a joke.

I can't believe this whole problem started because I spilled a can of brown paint back in third grade.

I don't know what to do, but I know I've got to do something.

What do you think I should do?

MORE TO THINK ABOUT:

- What do you think Casey should do? Why?
- Why do you think Heather treats Casey the way she does?
- How do you feel about Heather and her friends?
- Do you think the spilled paint is really the problem?

TRADING PLACES:

- If you were Casey, how would you feel and what would you do?

CRAZY CRITTERS
AND CREEPY CRAWLIES

There's "weird" and then there's "really weird." Duncan is definitely in the latter category.

Hi, my name is Spencer, and to help you understand where I'm coming from, I'll do a fast rewind to last summer. That's when my best friend, Marcus, moved to Arizona.

Losing my best friend who lived next door was bad enough, but I figured things couldn't get any worse. Boy was I wrong!

July 1 came, and that's when my whole world crashed and burned. That's the day Duncan Porter moved in next door.

To tell you the truth, I was actually feeling kind of excited when I saw the moving van unload a boy's red ten-speed bike. It looked like someone close to my age was moving in. I knew no one could ever replace Marcus, but at least maybe I'd have someone to walk to school with.

For a few nanoseconds I was actually feeling pretty good, and then I met Duncan. Or to be totally accurate, I just about fell over him.

My dad and I were tossing the football back and forth in the front yard when one of his passes went sailing over my head, and I backed up to catch it. That's when I fell backward over this big bump which turned out to be Duncan.

Duncan was down on his hands and knees searching for bugs. That's right—bugs! It turns out that he has this huge bug collection which is really gross. Ugh!

I'm not afraid of bugs or anything, but I figure life is a lot better for everyone if all the bugs just stay outside where they belong.

Well, anyway, that was my first encounter with Duncan, and things just got weirder and weirder after that.

I found out that he's not just crazy about bugs. He also loves hunting for frogs in the local swamp.

And Duncan isn't the only one in his family who's weird. He's got a sister who's just as weird as he is. I call her "Jillian the Reptilian" because all she ever talks about is snakes. She loves snakes, and I mean she really LOVES snakes. Snakes are her life!

Duncan is just not a kid I would hang out with if I didn't have to. And until three weeks ago, I didn't have to.

But then my mom got this part-time job, and my whole world got turned upside down. Just like that, my whole entire life was changed forever. You might say it hit a new low.

Every Wednesday afternoon while my mom is working I am now officially stuck at Duncan's house.

And hanging out with Duncan means doing weird stuff I would never do in a hundred years. Make that a thousand years. Having Duncan in your life is like having someone plaster mustard on your peanut butter and jelly sandwich.

I'll show you what I mean. He's got his own TV in his room, but does he watch sci-fi stuff or cartoons? Nope, he watches stuff about the Revolutionary War on the History Channel.

And when he's not watching the History Channel, he's watching even weirder stuff on the Discovery Channel. Stuff about bugs and prehistoric creatures I've never even heard of.

Being with Duncan is like total torture. He's not only weird, but he's also slow. Really slow. It's like everything he does is in slow motion.

I guess he's just being careful, but it drives me crazy. Sometimes I think I'll be happy if I can just get him to speed up from snail to turtle.

And talking to Duncan is impossible. It's like trying to cut through another space dimension, so now I just try to zone out and think about other stuff when I'm stuck at his house.

Right now he's working on a bug exhibit for the school science fair tomorrow, and his bedroom looks like it's just been hit by a tornado.

He's got science books stacked in piles all over his room, and he's all hyped up about this book called *Bugs Then and Now*.

He's begging me to help him label all his little exhibits. I know if I don't help him, he'll never have his project ready by tomorrow, but there's no way I want to mess with those bugs.

What do you think I should do?

MORE TO THINK ABOUT:

- What do you think Spencer should do? Why?
- How do you feel about Spencer?
- Do you agree with Spencer that Duncan is "weird"?
- Do you only choose friends who are like you? Why or why not?

TRADING PLACES:

- Would you help Duncan with his bug exhibit? Why or why not?

COOL, COOLER, COOLEST!

Hi, my name is Stephanie, and I can still hear the kids laughing at me in our science lab when I dropped the bag of marbles I had brought for my special project, and they went rolling all over the floor. It was only thirty marbles, but it seemed like a thousand as Mr. Yates and I tracked them down one by one.

A few kids shifted nervously in their seats, but no one helped. They just sat there staring, like I was the scheduled entertainment for the day.

As I was returning the last marble to the bag, I heard some girl across the room say, "Not the sharpest tack in the box, is she?"

It was Cynthia Winston, one of the cool girls in our class. She wears the coolest clothes, she has the coolest parties, and she only hangs out with other cool girls. No one is cooler than Cynthia Winston.

But she was right! I wasn't the sharpest tack in the box. It wasn't just that I was new this year. The problem was that I never seemed to know what to say to the other kids. So most of the time I didn't say anything.

By lunchtime I was feeling like a big fat zero, but I let my

feet drag me down the hall to the lunchroom anyway. I figured things couldn't get any worse.

Wrong! I didn't see anyone I knew, so I ended up sitting at a table in the corner all by myself staring at my lunch tray and having my own private pity-party.

I was still staring at the Tuna Surprise on my tray when I felt a whack on my back and Jasmine, a girl from my social studies class, plopped down onto the bench next to me.

"I thought you might like some company," she said, plunking her tray down on the table. "Have you started your report on Japan yet? I thought maybe we could work on it together."

While Jasmine was rattling on about ideas for our social studies project, I was busy eyeballing her. She was wearing patched jeans and a sweatshirt with a huge peace symbol splashed across the front of it. She could have made two of me, maybe three. Not exactly one of the coolest girls in our class. No, Jasmine was most definitely not one of the cool girls.

While I was still busy eyeballing Jasmine, a thin, wiry girl with glasses and a mouthful of railroad-track braces from my art class plopped down on the bench across from us.

I knew her name was Callan, but I had never talked to her. Actually, I guess I had never really tried talking to anyone. I had been too busy being homesick for my old school.

While Callan carefully picked the olives off her pizza, I noticed that her fingernails were chewed right down to the quick. I had a feeling that Callan wasn't exactly one of the cool girls either.

While I tried to balance a glob of green Jell-O on my spoon, I listened while Callan told me how last year had been her first year at Emerson Elementary, and how it had taken her almost three months to make a friend.

"But then I took pity on her and invited her to my pizza party," Jasmine chimed in. "I've got to tell you, that girl was so quiet we thought her lips were stuck together with Velcro."

While Callan tried to tell me about their Wednesday-night youth group, Jasmine kept interrupting.

"You should come with us this Wednesday because we're

going to have a scavenger hunt. It's going to be a real blast, and we're going to make our own root beer floats afterward."

I had to admit the scavenger hunt sounded like a lot of fun, but if I hung out with girls like Jasmine and Callan, what would the cool girls think?

While I inhaled the rest of my Tuna Surprise, I discovered how much the three of us had in common. We all loved books, volleyball, and double-cheese pizza, and we all hated word problems, hockey, and spinach.

As I finished chugalugging my carton of milk, Jasmine repeated her question. "So do you want to go on the scavenger hunt next Wednesday with us or not?"

What do you think I should do?

MORE TO THINK ABOUT:

- What do you think Stephanie should do? Why?
- Do you think Cynthia Winston is "cool"? Why or why not?
- How do you feel about Jasmine and Callan?
- What does "being cool" mean to you?

TRADING PLACES:

- How do you think Stephanie felt when Cynthia referred to her as "not the sharpest tack in the box"?

WARNING:
MINEFIELD AHEAD!

'␣ve had problems before, but I never thought they'd spill over into cyberspace. My name is Kevin and I feel like I'm in the middle of a war zone.

It all started when some kids in my class posted an online poll to determine the ugliest, the stupidest, the fattest, and the geekiest kid in our school.

In the beginning only a few kids voted, but as more kids found out about it, the Web site became really popular. Kids talked about it every day at school, and pretty soon it seemed almost everyone was voting.

I ended up being voted "the geekiest kid" in the school, which was bad enough, but poor Melissa was voted "the ugliest kid."

That poll was only the beginning! Then someone made a Web page about me listing the ten reasons why I am a loser. Half the stuff they listed wasn't even true, but I guess they just wanted to make it sound as bad as they could.

There was also a place on the Web site where visitors could add their own comments, and it seemed that each comment was worse than the one before it. It was like a contest to see who could come up with the meanest, most hateful put-downs.

I know that some kids just added the mean comments to stay on the buddy list, but their words still hurt. The buddy list is a lot like a regular gang where you have to do what the gang leader tells you to do or you're out of the gang. Or, in this case, off the buddy list.

Now I'm getting all these hate e-mails and IMs which say pretty much the same things that were posted on the Web page. That I'm a "loser" and "dumb" and a whole bunch of other stuff that's even worse.

Even if I block the senders, they can always use other e-mail addresses or screen names to continue the harassment.

These cyber bullies are just like regular bullies except that you can't see their faces, which makes them even scarier. They could be anyone. They could even be your best friends playing a joke on you.

I found out that I'm not the only one getting trashed on the Internet. After my friend Taylor had a fight with one of her friends, her friend started sending her threatening e-mails and then started a nasty blog about her

Taylor told me it got so bad that she was afraid to even go online because she didn't want to see what was waiting for her there.

Then there was my cousin Gabriella. She told me how her friends hijacked her screen name and then sent embarrassing e-mails and IMs to guys pretending to be her. Her friends thought it was really funny, but my cousin was totally humiliated.

I also heard about a kid at another school who got it even worse. Someone posted a Web page about him that included not just put-downs and nasty rumors but also pictures.

What's really popular now is taking embarrassing photos with a camera phone in the locker rooms and restrooms and then posting the pictures on the Internet where they can be down-loaded by anyone and spread around the whole world.

I even heard about a kid who beat another boy in an online game, and then some of the boy's friends started sending the kid messages that they were going to beat him up.

What's really scary about these cyber bullies is that you

don't know for sure who they are because they usually do every-thing anonymously. It's hard to fight back if you don't know who you're fighting.

It's also scary because it's like these bullies can come right into your home, so that you don't even feel safe at home any-more. They can strike anywhere, anytime.

I hardly ever visit chat rooms anymore because of some of the "bash boards" I've seen. Kids can write anything they want to on those online bulletin boards, and I've seen a lot of really cruel stuff that's out there for the whole world to see.

I haven't told my parents because I'm afraid they might tell me I can't go online anymore, and IM-ing is a big part of my life.

I feel like I'm walking through a minefield, and I don't know what to do.

What do you think I should do?

MORE TO THINK ABOUT:

- What do you think Kevin should do? Why?
- Have you ever been a victim of cyber bullying?
- Have you ever been a cyber bully yourself?
- What do you think about cyber bullying?

TRADING PLACES:

- Have you ever felt like Kevin?

NOBODY LIKES NEW

My name is Tara, and you won't believe this new kid who joined our class this year. Her name is Nardia or Narnia or something like that.

I guess I wasn't really listening to her name when Ms. Hartman introduced her because I was too busy staring at her. The new girl was wearing this shiny gold blouse and this gold headband with little fake jewels stuck all over it.

Every day she wears these long skirts down to her ankles, and I bet she doesn't even own a pair of jeans. She's from some country I've never heard of, and I can't even begin to pronounce her last name.

She must think she's better than the rest of us because she always sits by herself in the lunchroom and brings her own lunch from home. I guess she doesn't think our food is good enough for her.

My friend Cassie has started a secret petition that some of the girls have already signed. If you sign the petition, you promise that you will have nothing to do with the new girl and you will just ignore her whenever you see her.

I haven't signed the petition yet, but I'm seriously thinking about it. But right now I've got more important things to think about.

It's almost time for us to draw names for our social studies partners, and I'm holding my breath. This is our big social studies project for the year, and your partner is really important.

Last year I had Ricardo for a partner, and we ended up with one of the best projects in the class. But the year before that, I had a kid who never opened a book, and it was like pulling teeth to get him to do anything. I ended up doing all the work for both of us.

This year we're studying other cultures, and I'm hoping I get either Erin or Natasha for my partner because we work really well together. I guess I'll be happy with whoever I get as long as it isn't the new girl.

When it's finally my turn to draw a name from Ms. Hartman's little black box, I hold my breath again and cross my fingers. When I glance down at the paper I've drawn, I can't believe my eyes.

NADIA! This is probably the worst day of my life! I still can't believe I've actually drawn her name. I am so busted!

Monday is our first meeting, and I am seriously considering not showing up for class. To be honest, I'm beginning to feel pretty sick for real.

When I finally do get to class, all the kids are already paired up with their partners, and Nadia is at a corner table waiting for me. She has some photographs spread out on the table and asks me if I would like to do our project on her country.

Great! Not only do I get stuck with the new girl, but now I'm going to get stuck with her country, too.

I stare at the photograph of her house where she used to live, and it's like culture shock for me. Her whole house could fit inside our living room, maybe even inside our kitchen. She's standing in front of her house holding the hand of her little brother, but neither of them looks very happy.

It's not that they look sad or anything, but they just don't look very happy either.

As we sort through her photographs, I get more culture shock. There are pictures of kids begging on the streets, and Nadia tells me that sometimes what the kids earn on the streets that day goes to support their entire family.

Toward the end of the hour, Nadia shows me a picture of her dad in a military uniform and explains that's why they had to leave their country. She tells me that when a new government took over, it was no longer safe for her family to stay there, so they left everything they owned behind and fled to the United States for refuge.

I had no idea Nadia had been through so much, and I thought about Cassie's petition. I knew I would never sign it now, but what about the other kids?

What do you think I should do?

MORE TO THINK ABOUT:

- What do you think Tara should do? Why?
- How do you feel about Nadia?
- What do you think of Cassie's petition?
- How do you treat "new kids"?

TRADING PLACES:

- Have you ever been the "new kid" in the class? How did you feel?

ONE, TWO, THREE, AND COUNTING

My name is Elliot, and I'm still staring at the last page of my yearbook. Someone's written in huge letters:

TO THE FATTEST KID IN THE WORLD!

I don't know who wrote it because our yearbooks just get passed around while everyone signs. Then they get returned to us at the end of the day.

I can think of about ten kids who might have written it because kids have called me names since first grade.

I'm fat! I know I'm fat. The whole world knows I'm fat. I've tried to lose weight more times than I can count, but I always end up eating to make myself feel better.

It's a battle I can't ever win because it's a vicious cycle. I'm fat, so the other kids tease me. So I eat to make myself feel better, and then I just gain more weight and I end up being even fatter. And the kids tease me even more.

I've been teased just about all my life. In first grade the other kids used to follow me around saying "OINK OINK," and calling me "Mr. Piggy."

In second grade I hated recess because of the kids who

wouldn't let me swing on the swings or go down the slide. They told me that I might "break" them.

So I usually just stood there watching the other kids and waiting for the bell to ring. Sometimes it seemed like hours waiting for that bell to ring, so I could go back into the school.

In third grade kids told me I needed to lose weight to fit through the doors. And on the school bus, they pretended that the bus was dragging on the ground wherever I sat. That's when they began calling me names like "The Goodyear Blimp."

Fourth grade was no better. Kids still picked on me and made fun of me. Tyrone called me names like "Fatso" and "Fat-stuff," and sometimes I found pictures of pigs or hippos taped to my locker door.

Those names and pictures really hurt. They hurt a lot. I never cried at school, but I cried at home. I cried while I was taking a shower because I figured the water would wash away the tears and no one would know I had been crying.

Then this year in fifth grade some of the kids started passing notes around saying that I smelled and began calling me "Stinky."

One day in the locker room when I was changing for PE, three of the guys ran out of the locker room into the gym holding their noses and pretending they couldn't breathe because I smelled so bad.

Sometimes I wonder if maybe I do smell, so when I'm taking a shower at home, I scrub myself so hard that my skin gets red.

Changing in the locker room for PE class is bad enough, but the class itself is even worse. I'm just not any good at anything athletic.

I'm the first to peter out during laps on the track, the first to strike out during softball, and the first one to get "hit" with the dodgeball.

And, of course, I'm always the last one to get picked for a team. Any team. I can't say I blame anyone because if I were choosing a team, I wouldn't want me on my team either.

The other kids treat me like I have a force field around me

repelling anyone who gets close. Most of the time I feel lonely. Really lonely.

But I guess there are kids who have it even worse than I do. I heard about a kid whose bike got totally wrecked and left in pieces on his front porch.

And I heard about another kid who got stuffed into his gym locker by some of the guys on his soccer team.

So far no one's ever physically attacked me, but I've been threatened a few times, which is scary enough.

Sometimes I even think I deserve to be teased because I *am* fat and I *am* crappy at sports.

When I feel like I can't take any more and might just blow, then I make myself count to ten because I don't want to do anything I'll be sorry for later.

I really want to tell someone how I feel, but if I do, I'm afraid things might just get worse.

What do you think I should do?

MORE TO THINK ABOUT:

- What do you think Elliot should do? Why?
- Why do you think the other kids pick on Elliot?
- Have other kids ever teased you the way they tease Elliot?
- How would you treat Elliot?

TRADING PLACES:

- How would you feel if you were Elliot?

PAIN, PAIN, GO AWAY!

You should have heard that bang! That was Mariah slamming her locker door shut. That bang rattled every metal locker down the whole line.

Hi, my name is Haley and I know just how she feels. Last year that could have been me.

I will never, ever forget last year! That's when my life went from terrific to terrible to unbearable in just a few weeks. It became a never-ending nightmare!

Christmas vacation I was hanging out with my friends at the mall, sending e-mails back and forth, and things were like totally cool.

Then Christmas vacation was over, we were back at school, and I was suddenly being given the silent treatment. Believe me, I had no idea why my friends suddenly turned on me like that.

They stopped talking to me. They stopped calling. There were no more e-mails. And there was no room for me at their lunch table anymore.

The silent treatment was bad enough, but then came the whispering. Megan and Britney whispered things to each other, then stared at me and laughed. I knew they were talking about me, and I didn't know what to do.

Should I ignore them? Confront them? I felt totally helpless. My friends were suddenly no longer my friends, and I had no idea why.

Then came all the hate notes left on my locker door at school. I ripped the notes into tiny pieces and flushed them down the toilet. Then I watched them swirl around in the whirlpool of water. Going, going, gone!

But they weren't really gone. They weren't gone at all. Those notes were still very much alive and rolling around inside my head.

Kids even wrote hate notes on the windows of the school bus. Kids who used to be my friends drew pictures of me with their fingers on the frosted windows and then wrote things like HALEY IS UGLY or HALEY IS FAT.

And then came the crank calls. Kids would call at all hours of the day and night, and when I picked up the phone, there was nobody there.

Sometimes I could hear kids laughing on the other end of the line, and sometimes there was just total silence.

In the beginning, home had been my refuge. But now even my own home no longer felt safe to me.

I hated my life! I was tired of eating lunch by myself. I was tired of being teased and tormented. I was tired of trying to hold back my tears. And I was tired of teachers and parents telling me to just ignore the other girls.

Ms. Wilson, our guidance counselor, tried to help. She talked to the three of us, but Britney and Megan just looked really innocent and told her that they were just kidding around with me.

I think we all knew they weren't just "kidding around," but what could anyone do?

I always wanted to be popular and have a lot of friends, but I found out it's a lot better to have one friend you can trust than a whole lot of friends you can't trust.

This year I began hanging out with Tamika and Michelle. I pretty much ignored my old group and hardly ever even thought about them anymore.

Then tonight out of the blue Britney e-mails me and asks me to hang out at the mall with her after school tomorrow. She's got to buy a dress to wear to her sister's wedding, and she wants me to help her choose it.

My first thought is, *Not in this lifetime!* But then I begin remembering some of the great times we had together. All the overnights and summers at the lake. How we had shared all our secrets and promised to be friends forever.

Part of me wanted to get back together with my old friends, and part of me no longer trusted them.

And what about Tamika and Michelle? If I got back with my old group, would I have to dump Tamika and Michelle the same way I had been dumped?

What do you think I should do?

MORE TO THINK ABOUT:

- What do you think Haley should do? Why?
- How do you feel about Britney and Megan?
- Have you ever been "dumped" by a friend?
- Have you ever "dumped" a friend?

TRADING PLACES:

- How does it feel to be "dumped" or betrayed by a friend?

TRUTH OR DARE

T hree strikes and you're out! I guess that means me because this will be my third strike.

My name is Kyle, and I have a problem. A really big problem. I'm about to lose my best friend and probably get kicked out of the group of guys I hang with.

Last week it was **Strike One**. That's when my best friend, Daniel, dragged me over to Trevor's house for what he promised would be "a good time."

When we got there, Trevor and some of the other guys from my class were downstairs in his rec room all huddled in a circle. I could feel the hairs on the back of my neck begin to tingle, and I had a bad feeling.

I watched while Trevor inhaled a whiff of Dust Off and then passed the can to Ryan. I had heard about kids "huffing" before, but I had never seen anyone do it right in front of me.

And I knew kids who had sniffed stuff like glue and paint and gasoline, but I had never heard of anyone getting high from a can of computer duster.

Good grief, I had a can of computer duster sitting right next to my own computer at home. It's not like it's an illegal substance or anything. Anybody can buy a can anywhere.

Daniel was next to me waiting for his turn. "You have to try this," he said, grinning away. "This is just so cool and the stuff is really cheap."

When the can finally reached Daniel, he took a huge whiff and passed the can to me. I knew I couldn't do it, so I just passed the can on to Willis.

When I got home, I went straight to my computer. I avoided looking at the can of computer duster sitting there and looked up "inhalant abuse."

That's where I found out that what Daniel and the guys were doing is called "dusting," and what I found out really scared me. You inhale compressed air from a can of computer duster to get high, but you can end up dead!

I found out that inhaling the chemicals in a can of computer duster can give you a really great feeling for a few minutes, but you can end up with permanent brain damage or even dead.

I read story after story about kids who were permanently brain damaged or dead after "dusting." That was enough for me. I knew there was no way I was ever going to do it.

I even read about a kid who inhaled Freon from his home's air-conditioning unit and died instantly from "Sudden Sniffing Death Syndrome." His heart just stopped and he was dead.

When I told Daniel that inhaling the chemicals in computer duster could leave you with permanent brain damage or even kill you, he just laughed. He told me there was no way anything legal and so easily available could be dangerous. After all, you were just inhaling air.

I finally gave up arguing with him because I wasn't getting anywhere, and he ended up calling me names he had never called me before. Names that really hurt.

Then came **Strike Two**. Saturday night I was supposed to hang out with the guys at Daniel's house, but I told Daniel I couldn't make it because I had to watch my little brother.

I knew he didn't believe me, but I couldn't think of any other excuse at the time. I had some serious thinking to do, and I needed some time to do it.

I thought about my friends. They had been my friends for years, and I didn't want to lose them.

It's not like they're druggies or anything. Daniel and Ryan are always on the honor roll. Trevor's exhibits win a prize every year at the science fair. And Willis is the student government representative for our class.

I'm afraid that tonight it may just be **Strike Three**, which means I'll be out. Permanently out of our group.

Tonight is our regular meeting night, and Daniel made it very clear that I'd better be there. He told me that if I don't show up, he'll spread the word that I'm a total loser and a wimp.

I can't believe my best friend is doing this to me. It looks like a lose-lose situation no matter what I do.

What do you think I should do?

MORE TO THINK ABOUT:

- What do you think Kyle should do? Why?
- Why do you think Kyle's friends are abusing inhalants?
- Why do you think Daniel won't listen to Kyle?
- Do you think anyone else in the group feels like Kyle?

TRADING PLACES:

- Have you ever felt like Kyle?

SIMON SAYS

My name is Keisha, and I used to like my life! But that was "B.A." Before Andrea.

Andrea transferred to our school last month after she had some problems at her old school.

I know how hard it is to be the "new kid," so I tried to be really nice to her. I introduced her to my friends, and I invited her to eat lunch with us at our table.

I did everything I could to help her make friends and feel comfortable at our school. And, at first, everything seemed fine. Andrea liked my friends and my friends liked Andrea.

Then right after Thanksgiving everything changed, and Andrea became like a different person. Or maybe she was just showing us the real Andrea.

All I know is that my life suddenly went totally downhill and I no longer seemed to have any friends. Now *my* friends were Andrea's friends and I was no longer part of my own group.

No one from my group called me anymore, and when I called them, they were always "too busy" to do anything with me. I finally got the message loud and clear: I had been dumped!

When I confronted Andrea about being dumped by all my friends, she just smiled this weird little half smile and told me that I wasn't "black enough" to hang out with the African American clique. She said I acted and talked too much like a "white girl," whatever that meant.

When I tried talking to Letitia, she rattled off a whole list of really stupid reasons why I was out of the group. She even got on my case because I like rock music better than rap.

And when I ran into Trisha in the park, she told me flat out that she couldn't be my friend anymore because I no longer "fit in" with the other girls in the group.

I knew those were really Andrea's words, not Trisha's, but they hurt just the same. It seemed there was nothing I could do. Whatever Andrea wanted, Andrea got.

It looked like Andrea had convinced everyone in my group to dump me because now my group was *her* group and *I* was the outsider.

After that, there was no longer room for me at their lunch table. I no longer got invited to the overnights or the bowling parties or the pizza parties. No one even called me with any homework questions.

When I saw the girls from my old group talking in the hall, they suddenly got very quiet when I got close. And I could feel the temperature drop twenty degrees as I passed by them.

When I ran into any of my old friends at the mall, they just breezed right past me like they didn't even see me. And when I saw them together at the movies, I couldn't bear to look. I just wanted to disappear under the seats.

Not only was I OUT and Andrea IN, but it seemed she was calling all the shots. It was like Andrea was King of the Hill, and she made all the rules. If she said "jump," everyone jumped.

It was like she had brainwashed everybody, and everybody in the group just did whatever she told them to do with no questions asked.

Since I no longer had any friends to hang out with during lunch, I holed up in the library just reading and thinking.

I hate the word "clique." I never thought of my old group of friends as a clique, but I guess we were because we always hung out together and didn't mix much with the other kids.

After a while I made a few friends. Now I'm part of a new clique, but all the girls in this clique are girls who were excluded from all the other cliques.

We like each other for who we are and not for our looks, our clothes, the color of our skin, or our popularity. In my new group, no one tries to tell anyone else what to do or what to think, and I don't have to pretend to be someone I'm not. I can just be myself which feels pretty darn good.

I guess I could say I like my life again, but now I have a new problem. Yesterday Letitia asked me if she can join my new group because she wants to drop out of Andrea's group.

She told me that Andrea is too bossy and that she's tired of being told what to do all the time.

What do you think I should do?

MORE TO THINK ABOUT:

- What do you think Keisha should do? Why?
- How do you feel about Andrea?
- How do you feel about Letitia?
- How do you feel about Keisha's new group of friends?

TRADING PLACES:

- How would you feel if you were Keisha? Why?

OPERATION MELTDOWN

I hate broccoli. And I hate fractions. But most of all I hate my life. My life is like a bad dream. Correction: make that a nightmare!

My name is Cory, and I've decided that there are two kinds of people in the world: the bullies and the victims.

There's always that one kid in every school who gets made fun of and picked on. At my school, that kid is me.

I've been teased and bullied most of my life because of my learning disability. I'm not dumb or anything, but I do have to work harder than most kids just to get average grades.

I'm still called "sped" because I used to be in the special education class, which some kids call the "retard class." I'm not in the special education class anymore, but kids still call me "dumb" and "loser" anyway.

I used to hang out with a bunch of guys in my neighborhood, but they pretty much ignore me now. It's like I'm just not part of the group anymore.

I still remember the day last summer they went to the amusement park for the whole day, but no one asked me to go. They all talked about it afterward for what seemed like weeks. Maybe it was just days, but it seemed like weeks.

They probably think that if they hang out with me, then they'll end up on the "loser list," too.

It's pretty hard to stay neutral. Eventually you have to take sides, and you either side with the bully or you side with the victim. If you want to play it safe, then you side with the bully.

If you side with the victim, then there's a good chance you'll end up getting bullied, too.

For a long time I thought I was the only bully victim around here, but I found out I was wrong when I joined Ms. Wilson's group.

Ms. Wilson is our guidance counselor and she started a group for kids with school problems they want to talk about. At first I didn't want to sign up because I thought I'd be the only kid in the group.

It turned out there are five of us in her group, and I found out I wasn't the only kid being picked on.

Leah is Korean and she told us how she gets bullied almost every day. Some of the kids call her "Chink" and tell her she should go back to her own country. And some kids have even spit on her.

I always thought it was just the special ed kids who were picked on, but I found out I was wrong, wrong, wrong.

Warren is in all kinds of "challenge classes" because he's so smart. But I guess being really smart can make you a target for bullies, too.

Kids have taped "Kick Me" signs on his back, they have "accidentally" knocked him into the lockers, and they have dumped out his backpack in the trash barrels on the playground.

He told us that he spends 98 percent of his time obsessing about what to say and what not to say, so that he doesn't get teased.

He gets called names like "wimp" and "wuss," and he actually worries that if his grades are too good, he'll get picked on even more.

And there's Mariah. She told us how she's always wanted to be part of a group, but she's just never fit in. The kids call her "Mariah the Pariah" and make up really mean jokes about her.

She hates going to the lunchroom at noon because all the girls are sitting at tables with their friends, and there is never any room for her. They always tell her they're saving the empty seats for their "friends."

And then there's Elliot, who gets teased every day on the school bus. Kids call him names and hog all the seats, so that there's no place for him to sit down.

He says that now Felicia, the bus driver, has him sit up front with her, which is really embarrassing because the kids just tease him even more and call him "Felicia's Pet."

Every kid in our group feels really rotten, and we're all having mental meltdowns trying to figure out what to do.

What do you think we should do?

MORE TO THINK ABOUT:

- What do you think the kids in Cory's group should do? Why?
- How would you treat Cory and the other kids in his group?
- What do you think of Ms. Wilson's group?
- Does your school have a group like this?

TRADING PLACES:

- Have you ever felt like any of the kids in Cory's group?

SERIOUSLY UNCOOL

Jenna is nothing like me! That's why she's not my best friend. And that's why I only invite her over to my house if everyone else I know is busy. She is most definitely my last choice.

My name is Madison, and sometimes I think Jenna is from a different planet. Some kids call her "the drama queen" and some kids call her "the loser girl." That's because she just doesn't fit in with the rest of us.

Like when Lori and I are complaining about the last math test or cramming for a science test, Jenna is off in her own little world spouting off what Lori and I call her "foreignese."

Jenna is always saying stuff in French because she says that if she's ever going to be a foreign diplomat or an interpreter in a foreign embassy someday, she has to practice her French as much as she can.

Even in the lunch line, she says "merci" when the lunch lady hands her a carton of milk. This girl is like seriously uncool.

That's why I avoid Jenna 99 percent of the time. I only talk to her if no one else is around. And I only eat lunch with her if all the other tables are filled.

Then yesterday right out of the blue she asks me if she can

come to my karate class Wednesday to see what it's like. She's got to be kidding!

I can't really tell her she can't come because no one wants to hang out with her, so I kind of nod my head and mumble something I hope she can't understand.

But I guess she takes my mumbling for a yes because she

shows up at my house Wednesday afternoon after school, all ready to go to my karate class with me.

I've got to tell you, I'm beginning to come all unglued. It's not like I'm the coolest kid in the world or anything, but if I show up at karate with Jenna stuck to me, I will end up being labeled "loser girl" right along with her.

But what choice do I have? She's standing right here on my front porch waiting for me. So I grab my karate bag, and we head off to my class.

The whole three blocks to karate, Jenna is chattering away like she's just won the lottery while I'm busy trying to figure out how I'm going to lose her, so that at least we aren't walking in the front door together.

Too late! Mr. Desmond is already at the door welcoming all the kids, and Jenna pipes up and tells him she's my friend.

I am so dead! For the rest of my life I will be known as Jenna's friend, the loser.

Just as I'm thinking that things can't get any worse, my life hits rock bottom! Mr. Desmond invites Jenna to join our class for the day, and he even gives her a karate uniform to wear. I can't believe this is really happening.

Not only has Jenna maneuvered her way into my karate class, but she is wearing a karate uniform like all the rest of us. This is just so wrong!

I see Erica staring at me like she can't believe her eyes, and Nigel is giving me the old finger-across-the-throat sign. That's two friends down the drain just like that.

I can hardly wait till tomorrow. After Erica and Nigel spread the news that I brought Jenna to karate, I will have zero friends.

Mr. Desmond introduces Jenna to everyone in the class as my "friend" while I cross my fingers and hope that Jenna won't do anything really weird.

After Mr. Desmond demonstrates our three basic punches, he tells us to choose partners, so we can practice the punches.

Jenna is on the other side of the room trying to retie her karate belt, and if I'm ever going to ditch her, this is the time.

All I have to do is choose a partner. Any partner but Jenna. Then maybe she'll finally get the idea that she's not wanted here. And that she's not anybody's friend!

Oh, oh, she's spotted me. Here she comes headed right for me with a big smile on her face.

What do you think I should do?

MORE TO THINK ABOUT:

- What do you think Madison should do? Why?
- How do you feel about Jenna?
- How do you feel about Madison?
- Do you think Jenna knows how Madison and her friends feel about her? Why or why not?

TRADING PLACES:

- If you were Jenna, how would you feel if no one chooses you to be their partner?

SNAP, CRACKLE, POP!

My name is Tyler, and I used to like school. That is before I told my friend Spencer that I see a shrink, and he blabbed the news to every kid in our whole school.

I see a shrink once a week to help me deal with my cousin's death. My cousin and I were really close, and when he died of bone cancer last year, it was like a little part of me died, too.

I think talking to my shrink helps, but now I have a new problem because of Spencer and his big mouth.

At first, the other kids treated me like I had something "contagious" and just avoided me. No one sat with me at lunch, and when I passed kids in the hall, they just looked right through me like I was invisible.

Even my old friends stopped hanging out with me. It's like everything changed overnight. One day I had friends, and I had a regular life. And the next day I had zero friends, and I no longer had a life.

Everyone just stopped talking to me cold turkey with no explanation. I guess they figured it was no longer cool to hang out with me.

No one called me or e-mailed my anymore. And when I tried calling them, they were always "too busy" to do anything. There were days when I didn't talk to anyone.

After a few weeks of being ignored and avoided like the plague, I got the message loud and clear. My old life was gone, and now I was alone.

Being excluded and alone like that was bad enough, but now some of the kids are picking on me and giving me a really hard time.

They think anyone who sees a shrink must be really crazy, and they call me names like "psycho" and "wacko."

When they pass me in the hall, they do stuff like pretending to slit their wrists. And they write graffiti about me in the boys' bathroom.

Lately they've been taping pictures to my locker. They're usually pictures of scary monsters with my name on them. And once there was a picture of my soccer team with my face cut out of the picture.

I don't know which is worse—being ignored like I'm invisible or being taunted and humiliated. I guess maybe now I'd settle for being ignored.

After school, I usually hole up in my room and punch out my pillow. That makes me feel better for a few minutes, but then I just begin feeling angry all over again.

Last Tuesday I just couldn't take it any more, and that's when I came up with the idea of my "hit list." I actually wrote down the names of the five kids who torment me the most, and that was my secret hit list.

I don't know why, but somehow just making that list made me feel better. It's like it gave me a feeling of power, so I didn't feel so helpless.

Sometimes I even think about bringing a gun to school like those guys at Columbine and killing everyone on my hit list. I figure if they think I'm so "psycho," then I may as well really *be* psycho.

I know I would never do that, but it still scares me to know that I've thought about doing it.

I even have these fantasies about the kids who torment me. I pretend they're all on a school bus that rolls over a cliff. I don't really want them to get killed. I just want them to leave me alone.

It's like I have all this anger building up inside me, and I don't know what to do with it. Sometimes I feel like a keg of dynamite that's just waiting to be detonated.

What if someday I crack up and just pop like a balloon?

I know I would never do anything like what happened at Columbine, but it still scares me because I'm not sure what I might do.

So far I haven't told anyone how I feel because it might scare them, and then I could really be in big trouble.

What do you think I should do?

MORE TO THINK ABOUT:

- What do you think Tyler should do? Why?
- Why do you think his old friends have dropped him?
- Why do you think some of the kids are giving him such a hard time?
- What do you think of Tyler's "hit list"?

TRADING PLACES:

- If you ever felt like Tyler, where would you go to get help?

FOR THE SAKE
OF THE TEAM!

"P-l-e-a-s-e think about it!" Kelsey was pleading for the zillionth time. "Alyssa, we really need you. We can't do it without you. If you don't do it, we can't enter the competition!"

Hi, I'm Alyssa, and I *had* thought about it. I had thought about it every day for the last week. And as I replayed the last week in my head, I winced at the images.

Monday, the sign-up sheet went up on the activity bulletin board in the hall next to the gym.

COME ONE, COME ALL
ENTER THE DEBATE COMPETITION!
RULES ARE EASY:
TWO TEAMS, TWO DEBATERS PER TEAM
MAXIMUM TIME FOR EACH DEBATE:
FIFTEEN MINUTES
IT'S EASY, IT'S FUN, AND THERE WILL BE
PRIZES TO BE WON!

Kelsey had jabbed me in the arm. "Come on, this will be so fun, we've got to do this!" Those were her last words as she dragged me over to the table and signed us all up.

Easy for her to say, she was great with words. She could talk nonstop all day without taking a breath. Me, I'm your generic bookworm, and words just don't come easily to me.

I wasn't having a complete meltdown yet because I figured I could always come down with something serious but not too terminal at the last minute. Like maybe a bad case of laryngitis.

Then the tape began rolling through my head again and paused on Tuesday. By this time, Kelsey had Brianna and Lisa all fired up, and all three were like totally brainwashing me.

I tried to tell them there was no way I was going to get up on that stage and make a complete fool of myself. I still remembered how Kelsey had convinced me to try out for the drama club last spring. Just remembering those tryouts started sweat pouring down the back of my neck.

When I got up on that stage, my knees turned to Jell-O, and my mouth felt like it was stuffed with a whole bunch of cotton candy.

And when I tried to read the script, my hands were shaking so badly, the words just all blurred together like some Egyptian hieroglyphics. Talk about bad days!

For weeks after that, Tyrone and his friends made my life totally miserable. Every time they saw me, they grabbed their throats and pretended to be choking. Then they would just crack up laughing.

It got so bad that when I saw them coming, I ducked into a classroom just to avoid running into them.

I was still sweating bullets remembering those drama club tryouts when the tape in my head began rolling again and halted abruptly on Wednesday.

That's when Kelsey, Brianna, and Lisa cornered me in the lab after school and showed me the printed program. There were eight debates, and our team was third on the program.

If you're not shy like me, then you probably won't understand why I'm making such a big deal out of this. But, if you are shy, then you'll understand.

By the time the tape rolling through my head wound down to Thursday, I knew I was doomed and there was no way out. If I dropped off the team, then my whole team would have to drop out of the competition.

So anyway now it's Friday, and that's why I'm sitting here in the lunchroom counting the water spots on the ceiling while Kelsey reads off the list of official debate rules to me.

She tells me that each debate foursome will draw a topic out of a hat. Great! That means I won't even know what I'll be debating ahead of time.

Then each team will be given five minutes to decide which two members of the team will be "pro" and which two will be "con." Once the debate begins, each team will have exactly fifteen minutes to try to prove their case and then give their concluding remarks.

I squeeze my eyes shut, hoping Kelsey and her list of rules will disappear, but when I open them nothing has changed. Kelsey is still sitting there waiting for me to sign on the dotted line.

What do you think I should do?

MORE TO THINK ABOUT:

- What do you think Alyssa should do? Why?
- How do you feel about Tyrone and his friends?
- Why do you think they tormented Alyssa the way they did?
- How do you feel about Kelsey?

TRADING PLACES:

- Why do you think Alyssa still remembers Tyrone's harassment almost a whole year later?

WHEN ALL ELSE FAILS!

Why do you torment me
and cause me so much pain?
Why do you torment me
and call me ugly names?

Sometimes I think the pain I have
is just too much to bear
and if I were no longer here
would anybody care?

All I know for sure is
that I never did belong
but I just don't understand
What I did that was so wrong.

My name is Justin and I wrote that poem. That's what I do when I feel bad. I write poems or stories about how I feel. Sometimes writing makes me feel better and sometimes it doesn't.

I hate my life, and I mean I *really* hate my life. I hate my life because I hate school. And I hate school because of what happens at school.

I've been teased and bullied most of my life because I just don't fit in. I guess you could say I've never fit in.

I'm not like the other guys and I know it. They like games like football and soccer and basketball, and they like to play rough. Really rough.

Me, I like games where you have to think like chess and Scrabble. And I like music. I play the flute in the school band, and I love going to rock concerts.

I've never been any good at sports. I strike out in softball every time I'm up to bat, and I'm no better at soccer. I can't even hammer a nail without smashing my finger, let alone coordinate all my body parts to move a soccer ball up and down the field.

To be popular you have to act tough, be good at sports, and avoid "girly" things like playing the flute.

Some of the guys call me "band fag" because I play the flute, and last year Larry and some of his friends tossed my flute into the school dumpster. It was still in its case, so it didn't get hurt, but it was pretty humiliating having to climb into the dumpster to get my flute.

I guess kids consider me an easy target because I never fight back. So they just do whatever they feel like doing whenever they feel like doing it.

They trip me in the halls, they write all over my notebooks, and they call me names like "wuss" and "girly boy."

It's like I'm wearing a sign that says:

TORTURE AND HUMILIATE JUSTIN DAVIS!

Art used to be my favorite class, and I could spend hours working on a drawing. But now every time one of my drawings gets chosen to hang on the wall in the school office, I know it means I'll be in for a rough time. More name-calling. More pain.

When I was in first grade, I actually believed that old rhyme.

Sticks and stones may break my bones,
but names will never hurt me.

But I know better now. Words *can* hurt and they can hurt a lot.

The other kids make me feel like I'm a real loser. Like there must be something wrong with me.

Last week on the school bus Larry told me I should do us all a favor and kill myself. He even told me how I should do it.

I can still hear his words. It's like they're permanently recorded in my head where I hear them over and over again.

I know a girl who cuts herself because she says that when she's thinking about her physical pain, she's able to forget about her emotional pain.

I know how she feels because sometimes you just want to do anything you can to find relief from all the pain. I have thought about killing myself a few times. And I've even thought about how I would do it.

But I know that I don't really want to die. I just want the pain to stop.

What do you think I should do?

MORE TO THINK ABOUT:

- What do you think Justin should do? Why?
- Why do you think the other kids torment Justin?
- Do you think Justin is really a "loser"?
- How do you feel about Larry?

TRADING PLACES:

- If you ever felt like Justin, where would you go to get help?

GOING, GOING, GONE!

've lost my best friend, and it's totally my fault. My name is Morgan, and I wish I could erase last week from my life!

Kayla has been my best friend, sometimes my *only* friend, for two years now. We've never been part of the popular group, but it didn't matter because we had each other.

Well, last week I guess I kind of went a little crazy because the most popular girl in our class actually talked to me.

Her name is Cassie, and she is like totally cool. Well, anyway, during our gym class, Cassie and I were on the same volleyball team and she told me she wanted to talk to me later.

I've got to tell you, I was practically bouncing off the walls I was so happy. The most popular girl in our class wanted to talk to me after class. How cool was that!

Well, things got a little *less* cool after I found out what she wanted. She told me that I could be part of her group if I dumped Kayla.

I had no idea why she wanted me to dump Kayla, but without even thinking, I agreed to do it. Kayla had always been a good friend, and I liked her a lot. But there was no way I could pass up this chance to be part of the popular group.

Everyone else had finished dressing, so Cassie and I were

alone in the locker room. That's when she told me I had to dump Kayla if I wanted to be part of her group.

It's like I was hypnotized or something because Cassie just kept talking, and I just kept nodding yes. I think if she had asked me to jump out a window, I would have still been nodding yes.

Cassie told me that her group was the most popular group in

the whole school, but, of course, I already knew that. She told me how any girl in our whole school would die to be part of her group and, of course, I already knew that, too.

So anyway, Cassie kept talking and I kept nodding. It was like everything was a dream. I couldn't believe my whole life had changed like that in just a few hours.

When Cassie invited me to eat lunch at "her" table, I almost asked her if she was kidding. But, of course, I didn't. I just nodded that I would be there.

Kayla and I have walked by Cassie's table so many times and wondered what it would be like to sit there. What it would be like to be part of the popular group.

Now I would be one of the popular kids, and the other kids would be seeing me with new eyes. I was leaving Kayla behind, but that wasn't my fault. Cassie hadn't left me any choice.

It still didn't seem real when I joined Cassie and her friends at noon. I felt like I had died and gone to heaven.

Then I saw Kayla heading toward our table with a confused look on her face. Like she couldn't believe it either. Just as she got close to our table, Cassie moved her books over to cover the only empty spot on the bench and told Kayla, "There's no room at this table for you!"

I had no idea Cassie was going to do that. I don't know what I thought she was going to do. I guess I really hadn't thought about it all that much.

I didn't know what to do, so I didn't do anything. I just sat there staring at my plate like I was invisible.

I'll never forget that look on Kayla's face as long as I live. She had been betrayed by her best friend. She knew it, I knew it, and now everyone in the whole lunchroom knew it.

As Kayla dumped her tray on the counter and rushed out of the lunchroom, I just sat there not knowing what to do or say.

Then Cassie turned on me and said, "Run along after your friend, Morgan. You didn't really think we wanted you to be part of our group, did you?"

It took me a minute to really get it. Cassie had used me to humiliate Kayla, and now she was humiliating me, which I guess was her plan right from the start.

I had really messed up big-time. I had gone from having one friend to having no friends in less than five minutes.

It's been a week now, and Kayla still refuses to talk to me. I don't think she plans to ever speak to me again.

What do you think I should do?

MORE TO THINK ABOUT:

- What do you think Morgan should do? Why?
- How do you feel about Morgan?
- How do you feel about Cassie and her friends?
- Do you think Kayla will ever forgive Morgan? Why or why not?

TRADING PLACES:

- If you were Kayla, what would you do? Why?

HOW DO YOU
SPELL B-U-L-L-Y?

Hi, my name is Larry, and you've probably heard a lot of bad stuff about me. Well, I want to set the record straight. I don't do anything to anyone else that hasn't been done to me.

Okay, so maybe I do pick on the littler kids like Evan and Justin. But that's just what guys do. That's what the other guys did to me when I was in first and second grades, and I survived.

I was a skinny little kid back then, and the fifth and sixth graders shoved me around and called me names all the time. I got pushed off swings, I got knocked down, and one kid even wrecked my skateboard.

But did I fall apart like Evan does when the guys pick on him? No way! It toughened me up, so I'm the guy I am today. I'm a lot bigger now, and no one tangles with me. They know better.

Boys are supposed to act macho if they want to be cool. That's just the way it is. If you don't act tough, guys will think you're a wuss and then you'll get picked on plenty.

I learned the "guy rules" a long time ago from my friends. You have to act tough. You have to be good at sports. And you never show your real feelings. Especially if you're hurting.

That's where Evan really messes up because he ends up coming totally unglued every time he gets teased. It's so easy to make him mad. All you have to do is call him a name or give him a little shove.

Then he just gets madder and madder until he finally

explodes. One of these days he's going to burst into tears right in front of everyone, and that will be the end of Evan.

That's what happened to Justin. He couldn't take the teasing, and he just wimped out. Nobody likes a loser, and Justin is such a loser.

He never has been a regular guy and he never has fit in with the rest of us. Regular guys don't play the flute in the school band. Regular guys don't write poetry. And regular guys are tough, not athletic wimps like Justin.

We tease Evan because he gets so steamed that he looks like he's going to fall apart, and we tease Justin because he never fights back.

Like the time I threw Justin's flute in the school dumpster, and we all stood there laughing our heads off while he climbed in and got it. He didn't get mad, he didn't say anything. He just climbed into that dumpster and rescued his old flute.

That's what I mean about Justin not fitting in. A guy has to know how to fight back. You can't be a wuss or you're just asking to get picked on.

That's why one day on the school bus, I told Justin he should do us all a favor and just end it all. I even told him how he could do it. I didn't really mean it. I just wanted to see if I could get some kind of reaction out of him.

Like I said before, a real guy would have told me off or punched me out. But Justin just sat there and didn't say anything. Not one word. It's like he didn't even hear me.

That's why I pick on these guys. They let me do whatever I want, and they never fight back.

This is my best year yet. As a sixth grader, I'm at the top of the heap, and I can do pretty much whatever I want to anyone. That means I can choose who gets picked on and who doesn't.

I like that feeling of power. I like knowing that my friends will do whatever I do. If I pick on Evan, they pick on Evan. And if I pick on Justin, they pick on Justin.

Next year in junior high I may end up at the bottom of the heap, so I figure I may as well have some fun this year.

Last week we saw a film on bullies, and after the film, some of the guys told me that I was a lot like the bully in the film.

The bully's name was Leon, and I am nothing at all like him. Leon was a really mean kid, who totally terrified all the other kids in his class.

I know that some kids call me a bully, but I only pick on those kids who need to be toughened up, and I don't think anyone's afraid of me. They could fight back if they really wanted to.

You don't think I'm a bully, do you? Some kids tell me I should back off a little.

What do you think I should do?

MORE TO THINK ABOUT:

- What do you think Larry should do? Why?
- Do you think Larry is a bully? Why or why not?
- What do you think about Larry's "guy rules"?
- What is a "bully"?

TRADING PLACES:

- How would you feel if you were Evan or Justin?

A FINAL NOTE

I hope your visit with the students at Emerson Elementary School has given you a number of things to think about.

These stories could be stories from any elementary school anywhere or maybe even from your own local middle school or junior high.

You don't have to be "best friends" with everyone, but you can still treat everyone with respect and courtesy.

So let's begin today to treat others the way we would like to be treated. We can do this by following the words of Dr. Martin Luther King Jr.:

"The time is always right to do what is right."

BULLYING STATISTICS

- Bullying has been identified as a major concern by schools across the United States. (National Education Association, 2003.)
- According to the National Association of School Psychologists, five million elementary and middle school students in the United States are bullied each year, and each day bullies' teasing leads some 160,000 fearful kids to skip school. (Elizabeth Siris.)
- Studies show that between 15 and 25 percent of US students are frequently bullied while 15–20 percent report that they bully others frequently. (Stop Bullying Now!)
- US Department of Education statistics show that the incidence of behaviors such as bullying increased by 5 percent between 1999 and 2001, and in 2001, 8 percent of students reported that they had been bullied at school within the last six months. (Wellesley Centers for Women.)
- The results of one poll found that one-third of all teens polled (ages twelve to seventeen) and one-sixth of children polled (ages six to eleven) have been victims of cyber bullying. (Opinion Research Corporation.)

- It is estimated that one out of ten students who drop out of school do so because they are the victim of repeated bullying. (Michael Wellins.)
- Bullying in schools is a serious problem which can result in the victims becoming depressed, sometimes so depressed that they think about taking their own lives. (Kevin Caruso.)

WEB SITE REFERENCES

Caruso, Kevin. "Bullying and Suicide." Prevent Suicide Now.com. June 16, 2006. http://www.preventsuicidenow.com/bullying-and -suicide.html.

National Education Association, 2003. "National Bullying Awareness Campaign." http://www.nea.org/schoolsafety/bullying.html.

Opinion Research Corporation. "CYBER BULLY: PRE-TEEN." Prepared for Fight Crime: Invest in Kids, July 6, 2006. http://www .fightcrime.org/releases.php?id=231.

Siris, Elizabeth. "The Bully Battle." In *Time for Kids* magazines 6, no. 7 (October 27, 2000). http://www.timeforkids.com/TFK/magazines/ story/0,6277,58168,00.html.

Stop Bullying Now! "What We Know about Bullying" fact sheet. September 11, 2006. http://www.stopbullyingnow.hrsa.gov/adult/ indexAdult.asp?Area=whatweknow.

Wellesley Centers for Women. "Facts about Bullying." June 16, 2006. http://www.wcwonline.org/bullying/facts.html.

Wellins, Michael, Orange Police Department Crisis Intervention Specialist. "Bullying: A Presentation of Information and Strategies." June 16, 2006. http://www.orangeusd.k12.ca.us/cwa/Part%201%20BULLYING-PTA-2005-NO%20PICS.ppt.

AFTERWORD

Bullying was once considered a character-building rite of passage for our children. But now it is seen for what it is—a form of victimization and abuse.

Bullying behavior can be defined as a variety of negative aggressive acts that are intentional and are repeated over time to inflict pain or discomfort, humiliate or embarrass, or create fear in the person being bullied. Bullying behavior involves a real or perceived imbalance of power, with the more powerful individual or group attacking those who are seen to be vulnerable or powerless. Examples of bullying behavior include physical acts (hitting, kicking, spitting, or pushing); verbal aggression (taunting, malicious teasing, name-calling, spreading rumors, threatening, or cyber bullying); or psychological abuse (manipulation of social relationships, destroying another's reputation, threatening gestures, promoting social exclusion, extortion, or intimidation).

Bullying creates a climate of fear that makes students feel unsafe. It is important that students recognize that they, along with their parents and teachers and school administrators, are responsible for helping to create a safe, caring, respectful school environment. Without having empathy for the feelings and safety of others, we can let the bullies take over the school—and poison the school's social and learning environment.

Researchers have found that peers are present in 85 percent of bullying episodes but only intervene to stop bullying 10 percent of the time (Atlas and Pepler 1998). Ninety percent of those who observe bullying say that they find it an unpleasant and disturbing behavior to watch (Ziegler and Pepler 1993).

When you are a bystander in a bullying situation, what are your choices? The Olweus Bullying Circle, developed by Dan Olweus, PhD, of the University of Bergen, Norway, explains the various roles that people play in a bullying situation. There are specific roles for those who bully, those who are bullied, and the bystanders (Olweus 2001).

Generally, there are four roles that bystanders can choose to play:

(1) You can choose to join in the bullying to become an assistant or "henchman" supporter of bullying. You can become actively involved and provide physical, verbal, or psychological assistance to support the bully. (This may assure you a position in the bully's inner circle.) (2) If you don't want to actively participate in the bullying, but you still want to be in the good graces of the bully, you can choose to be a bullying "supporter" by providing an audience for the bully and act like what the bully is doing is OK. Perhaps you can even "admire" the bully and try to imitate his or her behavior in your dealings with weaker individuals. (3) You can choose to pretend to be an outsider or a disengaged onlooker whose motto is "It is none of my business" and disengage from any responsibility for the bullying situation. (4) You can choose to become a defender of those individuals who are being bullied.

Victims are often reluctant to report bullying and may need your help to get the bullying to stop. It is important for you to understand that many victims don't report being abused to their parents or teachers because they're embarrassed or humiliated by the bullying. They may assume that adults will accuse them of tattling or will tell them to deal with the bullying on their own. Some victims believe there is nothing adults can do to get the bully to stop. If the bullying continues and friends don't step in to help, the victim may eventually believe that they deserve this kind of treatment by others—starting a lifetime of victimization by those more powerful.

Most people are uncomfortable and feel like they ought to help those who are being bullied, but bystanders often fear the bully as well. Those watching the bullying may be afraid of becoming the next target if they try to help or they may fear that they will make the situation worse for the person being bullied. Sometimes you may just not know what to do. By remaining silent or doing nothing, however, your inaction signals to the bully that you think the bullying is all right.

Being alert and observant to what is going on around you is critical if you want to end bullying in your school. There are some "cool" things you can do to help those who are being bullied.

- Realize that nobody "deserves" to be bullied by others. Do not rationalize a bully's cruel behavior as being something that another person deserves.
- Try not to take part in the bullying and don't encourage the bullying by watching or helping the bully.
- Try not to repeat the gossip a bully is spreading about another classmate.
- Don't stand by and watch bullying take place or say things that encourage a bully to act. The bully wants and needs an admiring audience to gain power.
- Reach out to those who are being bullied.
  - * Invite them to join your group when you are talking with your friends.

* Include them at your table at lunch.
* Talk with them whenever possible and get to know them as individuals.
* If you feel comfortable, tell them that you saw the bullying incident and that you are sorry it happened to them.
- Talk to your friends about your concerns about bullying and join with them to become peaceful individuals who do not participate in bullying situations.
- Tell adults at school what you saw happen in the bullying situation and expect them to act on your report.
- Tell your parents when you observe bullying.
- If the bully is your friend, try to get him or her to stop bullying others.

You should expect the following from your school:

- Written school policies and rules against bullying, harassment, and intimidation should be in place—and be enforced.
- School administrators, teachers, and staff should take bullying problems seriously. The school should investigate the situation and let you know what steps they're taking to help stop the bullying.
- Teachers and administrators should speak to the bully and his or her parents. They should also tell the bully what the consequences will be if he or she doesn't stop bullying others. If the bullying continues, the school should enforce the predetermined consequences immediately.
- Teachers and administrators should increase adult supervision in the areas of the school campus where bullying incidents are most likely to occur.

- School personnel should be well informed about the dynamics of bullying behavior so that they can monitor and provide support to all students as needed.
- School personnel should communicate often with parents of those involved in bullying situations to let them know how the situation is being handled at school.

BUILDING A BULLY-FREE FUTURE

Even though bullying has existed in schools for decades, that is no excuse to continue to allow students to be bullied. Researchers have gained new understanding of the dynamics of bullying and the roles of all those involved. The long-term negative outcomes of individuals who are bullied as well as for those who are allowed to bully others and those who watch it happen are too serious to ignore.

Adult commitment to ending bullying in schools is critical (Limber and Snyder 2006). In many cases, it will be the parent who must take charge of bringing the bullying incidents to the attention of school authorities. Parents should expect full cooperation from the school to resolve the problem. Educating children about bullying behavior and the roles they may choose to play as a bystander offers children the opportunity to act to defend social justice, but adults must take responsibility for providing the structure to end bullying at school. Children must have faith that the adults in their environment will act to protect them and keep them safe in all circumstances.

Many schools throughout the world have successfully implemented bullying prevention programming to provide meaningful support to those who are bullied, opportunities for improved behavior for those who bully, and encouragement for bystanders to step in and speak out. The result of reducing bullying in our schools is an improved school environment that is friendly and welcoming to all students.

In schools where children feel protected from bullying behaviors, they are free to spend their days learning, building friendships, and exploring all the possibilities for their lives.

REFERENCES:

Atlas, R., & D. J. Pepler. 1998. "Observations of Bullying in the Classroom." *American Journal of Educational Research* 92, 86–99.

Limber, S. P., and M. Snyder. July 2006. "What Works and Doesn't Work in Bullying Prevention and Intervention." *The State Education Standard: The Journal of the National Association of State Boards of Education.* (Special Edition: Creating Safe Places to Learn.)

Olweus, D. 2001. *Olweus' Core Program against Bullying and Anti-social Behavior: A Teacher Handbook* (Version 3), chapter 3, p. 21. Center City, MN: Hazelden Publishing.

Ziegler, S., and D. J. Pepler. 1993. "Bullying at School: Pervasive and Persistent Special Issues: Violence in the Schools/Schooling in Violence." *Orbit 24*, 29–31.

RECOMMENDED WEBSITE RESOURCES:

Blueprints for Violence Prevention: http://www.colorado.edu/cspv/blueprints/index.html

International Bullying Prevention Association: www.stopbullyingworld.com

isafe America (Internet Safety & Cyberbullying Information): http://www.isafe.org/channels/?ch=ai

Model Bullying Prevention Program: http://www.colorado.edu/cspv/
   blueprints/model/programs/BPP.html
National Education Association on bullying: http://www.nea.org/
   schoolsafety/bullying.html
National Youth Violence Prevention Resource Center on Bullying:
   http://www.safeyouth.org/scripts/basicsearch/basicsearchresults
   .asp
Olweus Bullying Prevention Program: www.clemson.edu/olweus
US National Stop Bullying Campaign Educator's Corner: http://www
   .stopbullyingnow.hrsa.gov/adult/indexAdult.asp?Area=teachers
   corner
US National Stop Bullying Now Campaign: www.stopbullyingnow
   .hrsa.gov

Marlene Snyder, PhD, is National Olweus Bullying Prevention
Program Director at the Institute on Neighborhood and Family
Life, Clemson University, Clemson, South Carolina. She is an
international conference speaker and technical assistance con-
sultant for a wide variety of professional organizations
including the National Council of Juvenile and Family Court
Judges, the Office of Juvenile Justice and Delinquency Prevention, the Child Welfare League of America, and the National
Center on School Engagement. Dr. Snyder is the founding president of the International Bullying Prevention Association.

as his audience turned from all-age to global. He did not deliberately design the movies for a global audience, although he collaborated with international actors and writers. The change that starts even with *The Color Purple*, but more perceptibly with *Empire of the Sun*, is a shift from movies that flatter an American audience with self-portraits to those that present Americans in a context in which the international audience will be interested. It is a subtle, not an overt, response to the changing box office. It becomes the basis for moving away from right-wing ideology.

In 1985 Spielberg signed a contract with NBC to produce two years' worth of a television anthology show called *Amazing Stories*. His move into television demonstrated a shrewd instinct about the evolution of the small screen. The barriers between television and film that he had to overcome a decade earlier were coming down. Technology and the changing nature of daily life were forcing a convergence on the leisure industries. Cable and satellite delivery systems had changed the film world, as many executives had anticipated. However, the most important new technology, which Hollywood did not anticipate, was the VCR. These changes were all on the level of distribution and the ways people experienced films. Both film artists and business people could sense that the small and big screens were converging.

I have already discussed that Spielberg and his fellow directors were designing (consciously or unconsciously) for both screens at once. Why not actually use television to do the things that feature filmmaking could not do? Such as a smaller budget, shorter production times, a faster schedule, and the use of up-and-coming talent who had not yet proved themselves ready for the feature film. Spielberg got to choose actors, directors, and stories on relatively short notice. The anthology series aired a new half-hour story with new characters and a new director every week on NBC, starting in the last week of September 1985. The only continuing thread was that Spielberg was the producer, along with two veterans of the TV series *St Elsewhere* (NBC, 1982–1988): John Falsey and Joshua Brand.

For his own directing assignments he chose two episodes: "Ghost Train" (aired September 28, 1985) and "The Mission" (November 3, 1985). Both relied on magic and wish fulfillment. More interesting was that both revealed a frustrated historical imagination. "The Mission" was about a World War Two bombing mission where the tail gunner gets stuck in his bubble on the underside of the B-17. It allowed Spielberg to indulge in recreating scenes from the war movies of his youth. "Ghost Train" was an equally flimsy story, but it, at least, had the curious status of picking up a theme that had already been set up in *Poltergeist*. The key piece of villainy in the horror movie was that the developer built the houses on top of a cemetery that he did not bother to move. The threatening spirits came from the cemetery the developer had desecrated. This moral of the consequence of desecration was premised on the past adhering to the land.

In "Ghost Train" Spielberg uses this concept at greater length. The story revolves around a grandfather (Robert Blossoms) and his grandson (Lukas Haas). The grandfather had inadvertently caused a train derailment when he was the same age as his grandson is. Now he is old and the train tracks and any other physical reminder of the event are long gone. Nonetheless the grandfather recognizes that the derailment of his youth occurred on the very spot that the boy's family had built their ranch house. The old man senses the train will now come back to get him to take him to the next life and through magic it does so.

The thought that history adheres to the land can be traced back to eighteenth- and nineteenth-century European romanticism. Spielberg goes almost to the point of whimsy to find this romance in *Poltergeist,* and embedded in a Colorado cornfield in "Ghost Train." This is a well-honed sunbelt frustration at the limit of imagination in a new land. In "Ghost Train" this limit comes out in an exchange between the boy and his mother (Gail Edwards). The boy complains that no one will ride out to play with him because the house is too far away from his playmates. In his loneliness in this new land the child then pesters his grandfather to tell him about the Indians and their life on this part of the great American plains. History becomes a way to people the empty landscape and to relieve the boredom for both of them.

THE PULL OF HISTORY: *THE COLOR PURPLE*

Spielberg did not ask viewers to take either of the two TV episodes seriously as historical films. In "The Mission" he was interested in recycling old Hollywood images but there was not yet a vision of the moral problems of World War Two. In "Ghost Train" he only hinted at the power of the past.[15] He created a more determined opportunity to explore the past in his only feature film of 1985. *The Color Purple* was based on Alice Walker's best selling novel, which was popular, and suffiently literary, to win a Pulitzer Prize in 1983. Warner Studios had the movie rights and one of the producers attached to the novel was the famed musician Quincy Jones. He thought that getting Spielberg to direct would put the film into a higher financial category in terms of budget, marketing, and profitable returns. Spielberg's producer, Kathleen Kennedy, brought the novel to the film director's attention and Jones convinced him to stretch into new territories with this novel. Steven Ross, the CEO of Warner Communication, had already been cultivating Spielberg and was only too glad to assign the story to him, as soon as he expressed interest.

But the result was more myth than history. It was the first self-defined "serious" film by Spielberg but despite the seriousness he was obsessed with pleasing the audience. He was hampered by his position as a white director making a mass audience film located several decades previously in the African American community in Georgia. Nonetheless, the film managed to combine the wish-fulfillment yearnings of the film director with similar yearnings from the writer Alice Walker and from an African American audience. This was done despite the howls of protest from an intelligentsia who saw little reality in the fictionalized landscape.

The Color Purple is about African Americans in rural Georgia during the 17 years between 1909 and 1936. A young woman named Celie (Whoopie Goldberg) survives rape and abuse by her father (who is subsequently revealed to be her stepfather). Her children are given away; her only positive relationship is with her sister Nettie (Akosia Busia). Celie is married off to another abusive farmer, Mister (Danny Glover), and he banishes her sister Nettie after she refuses his sexual advances. Mister brings home his mistress Shug (Margaret Avery) who at first is unkind to Celie but subsequently teaches her to love and take pride in herself. Because of such mentoring Celie defies her husband and goes off to make her own living by tailoring. The story concludes as Mister realizes his error and pays for the return of Celie's children from Africa and the entire family reunites (except for Mister). Even he is a redeemed witness to the union.

When a white heterosexual male films a story about southern Black culture with important depictions of lesbianism and male control of women, he is courting controversy. Spielberg anticipated this and tried to forestall it with several strategies. He sought and won approval from the novelist Walker. She had her own strategy for positioning the film which included praising the young successful filmmaker for his treatment of

the extra-terrestrial as the outsider in *E.T.* Spielberg continued to defuse the issue by saying, "if the novel had been about
racial conflict, 'I wouldn't have been the right director for
the project and I would not have done the movie.'" He
explained his motivation for doing the film by saying that he
wanted to try character-driven drama to follow the examples
of Sidney Lumet, Sydney Pollack, and Paddy Chayefsky
(Bobo, 278–79).

At the time of the film's release in December 1985, network
television had been the more progressive medium and had
gone much further than the Hollywood film industry in por-
traying African Americans. The most notable treatment of
black history was one of the most highly rated TV shows of
all time, *Roots* (ABC, January 23–30, 1977). Despite the
success of *Roots*, filmmakers continued to avoid the theme on
the big screen. Closer in time to *The Color Purple* was another
television phenomenon. On September 20, 1984, *The Cosby
Show* premiered on prime time (NBC, 1984–1992) and its
setting of a contemporary African American family headed
by two successful professionals immediately attracted a huge
audience from every segment of American society. These
projects mirrored a new self-interest on the part of an emerging African American middle class. This audience was interested in family heritage stories. In a loose way *The Color
Purple* was looking for a middle-class audience analogous to
the middle-class viewers of British "heritage" films.

It succeeded in attracting a crossover audience and was
popular with both black and white Americans. *The Color
Purple* went on to global box office earnings of $142 million,
while its budget was only $15 million. Domestic ticket sales
accounted for two-thirds of its earnings ($94 million), which
placed it fourth for the year. It is curious that the film made
so much more money in North America than in the rest of
the world. This discrepancy supported the cliché, prevalent

in Hollywood at that time, that films with black actors received limited foreign interest. The cliché had become self-fulfilling since such films never received adequate overseas marketing budgets.[16]

Despite its popularity, *The Color Purple* did not win any Oscars for its director. The film itself lost out for best picture to *Out of Africa*, which ironically featured white colonialists in Kenya. The picture, conceived as marking the maturing of Spielberg as a director, was a courageous project to take on. The director, however, was not about to ask the audience to engage in equal acts of courage. He sweetened their passage through Celie's hard life. At every step he amplified the story's theme of self-empowerment and wish fulfillment. The audience was continually rewarded for identifying with Celie. The visual treatment was also designed to be a pleasing experience. In the film the farms were well manicured and lush. There was no hint that a harvest could fail. When questioned about the bucolic setting, Spielberg referred to Ms. Walker's own well-to-do rural grandparents as justification for the visual prosperity (Friedman, 259–60). He avoided poverty and class divisions and he kept the racial segregation off the screen except for one tragic encounter between Sophia (Oprah Winfrey) and the Mayor's wife.

Spielberg approached the past by recycling both the bad and good of old Hollywood. Whoopi Goldberg described how he directed her by asking her to imitate films that they both knew. His other attempts to find older models backfired; he upset Alice Walker by telling her how much he loved the character of Prissy (Butterfly McQueen) in *Gone With The Wind* (1939). As with the colonialism in *Raiders*, old Hollywood misled Spielberg about how to treat a segregated Georgia. His omissions and defensiveness showed that he had yet to realize why he wanted to make a history film.

In the same year, Spielberg produced a Robert Zemeckis film, *Back to the Future*, that was more interested in changing the past than questioning the present. A teenager goes back twenty years in time to give his father some moral backbone and save the future of his family. The analogy with the Reagan rhetorical reworking of the past was apparent. Zemeckis would continue in this vein, showing his contempt for the struggles of the 1960s in the openly reactionary *Forrest Gump* that he made in 1994. Although Spielberg never addressed his former protégé's politics, he was already turning away from Zemeckis's conservative revision by deciding to take a bolder step into historical realism and seek an international audience. In March 1987 Spielberg started filming a World War Two fictionalized memoir by J. G. Ballard entitled *Empire of the Sun*.

SPIELBERG'S FIRST HISTORICAL FILM

Empire of the Sun was an exploration of filmmaking not constrained by high concept and other marketing impulses. Spielberg wanted to explore this kind of filmmaking by replicating the films that he had watched as a child, such as those directed by David Lean, who brought J. G. Ballard's novel to his attention. Spielberg spotted a particularly visual story in the novel, which also furthered his own obsessive association of flying with freedom from family and social constraints. Ballard portrayed a boy fascinated by flight. In addition the World War Two setting was a good exercise for the film director, who was still contemplating the challenge of filming a story about Oskar Schindler as the savior of concentration-camp Jews. Another attractive factor was that it reminded Spielberg of one of his own childhood movie favorites, *Captains Courageous*. American interest in China had been growing since the economic liberalization of the post-Mao regime. Marketers could hope that this interest could transfer to a film about the Chinese experience of World War Two.

Action films were getting faster in their pacing and more extreme in their action. More and more the only visual pleasure in these films was the action itself. In contrast, there was an earlier model of spectacular films that found visual awe in the landscape, not in action. Spielberg was inspired by David Lean's epics dating from the road show era, and he had discussions with the 79-year-old Lean about who would direct the movie. Lean was a master of giving the audience powerful stories set against compelling landscapes. He had worked his way up the British filmmaking industry quickly and by the mid-1950s was able to get major funding from the Hollywood company Columbia to make *Bridge on the River Kwai*. Lean made two more major Hollywood films, albeit with British actors: *Lawrence of Arabia*[17] and *Dr. Zhivago*. Then his star turned when his next big-budget movie, *Ryan's Daughter*, faltered in 1970. He had to wait fourteen years to make his last film, *A Passage to India* (1984). In *Lawrence* and *Zhivago*, Lean attracted a mass audience for historical stories told across vast expanses of land. The main characters were men placed between different civilizations. The genre pleasures of watching a Lean movie are a shifting balance between landscape/action and romance.

The spectacle of landscape had been eclipsed in big-budget movie making by the mid-1980s. The Technicolor Western had disappeared. Only a few blockbusters would work outdoor vistas and epic sweeps into their high concept frames. Only directors with some clout could every so often get a studio to make such a film. Warren Beatty had to lobby for several years and had to use all his power as a preeminent movie star to finance his film—*Reds* (1981)—that featured a love story against the epic events of the 1917 Russian

Revolution. It was not a monetary success. Lawrence Kasdan cashed in the cultural capital he had earned on *The Big Chill* (1983) to make *Silverado* in 1985. This big vista western did not do well in the theater. Spielberg also had to use his own power to get *Empire's* large financing into place. The film was shot for a very large $38 million, 90 percent higher than the average major movie. Perhaps the Warner executives were inspired by the Italian-British-Chinese co-production of *The Last Emperor,* filmed earlier in 1987 for $25 million (Lev, 117). In any case they would not say no to Spielberg.

The story is about Jim Graham (Christian Bale), the 11-year-old son of an English businessman living in Shang-hai. It is 1941 and the Japanese have overrun the outskirts and are poised to take the city from the few Chinese defend-ers. In the chaos of their attack Jim is separated from his parents and has to fend for himself. He is alone in the city and soon falls in with two American lowlifes. The Japanese intern all three of them when they are caught on a foraging expedition. They are put in a labor camp full of interned Europeans and Americans. There they build an airstrip for the Japanese air force. The story jumps four years to the end of the war. Jim has learned to be a skillful survivor by emulat-ing the Americans more than the passive, demoralized British. The entire camp is abandoned by the Japanese as the war ends and Jim once again is left on his own until he is picked up by the American army and reunited with his parents.

There was less sugarcoating than *The Color Purple*, although the atrocities were kept mostly off-camera. The source mate-rial's hints of homosexual predations on the part of the Amer-ican lowlifes were totally expunged. This was Spielberg's first serious film with a foreign setting. *Empire* got twice as many foreign viewers as domestic. Was he actually following his audience by moving this film away from an American-centric view of the world? The film is completely centered on a colonial English boy who has never been in England. Neither his father (Rupert Frazer) nor Dr. Rawlins (Nigel Havers) can get Jim to express national loyalty. In the final scene of reuniting with his parents, he cannot recognize them. Jim Graham has become a young man without a home.

The film has a tendency to emphasize the Americans over the British or other groups (Gormlie). The lead American is Basie (John Malkovich), who is in the familiar line of American rogues with roots as far back as Mark Twain's King and Dauphin in *Huckleberry Finn*. Basie is a darker version of the American adventurer; he is a self-centered survivor whose only redeeming quality is the intermittent interest he takes in Jim. The movie soft-pedals Basie's actual betrayals. Jim is drawn towards Basie because of the older man's vitality, which he does not find among the others. But the vitality has little purpose and no accomplishment. Basie never gains control of a situation. It is Jim who can take over situations, whether placating the Japanese commander or hunting outside the fence for a bird to eat.

The audience did not see the film as a forceful statement on the American role in the world. The box office was disappointing and the reviews were mixed. The *Los Angeles Times* critic was irritated and wrote that "the film's grave problem is a lack of central heating. We don't have a single character to warm up to. They are either illegal, immoral or fatally malnourished" (Benson). *Empire* was too distant from the Spielberg brand name. It was Spielberg's first movie since *Sugarland* to have less than ten million American viewers; one-tenth of his average audience numbers. But others (particularly foreigners) realized that it marked Spielberg's emergence from the high concept trap, even though he had not been able to fully engage the American audience with the story.

Empire is Spielberg's first step from making films set in the past towards making historical movies. The happy ending is neither happy nor is it an ending. It is a prelude to a new more deracinated world where loyalties are not easily granted to nations or even to smaller groups. It is often considered a warm-up exercise for *Schindler's List*, but in many ways *Empire* is more demanding of an audience than Schindler. It does not offer redemption. The evil is more contextual, less obvious, particularly since neither Jim Graham not the audience of the movie witness the destruction of Shanghai. Horrible beauties are found in the remnants of immense tragedies such as caskets floating in the harbor; an implied rape in the footprints set in spilt talcum powder; the depiction of the distant Hiroshima bomb as a subtle colored light in the morning sky that Jim mistakes for a departing soul. Jim constantly looks to the Japanese as a group who can help him survive, not as a threat. In *Empire* it is not so clear that to survive is the highest good, as it is in *Schindler*. While viewers have witnessed the maturing of the boy, neither the filmmaker nor the audience were quite sure what the boy has learned.

Since Spielberg is telling a story with fewer moral certainties than usual, there is less immersion into the action by the camera. He has a harder time asking the viewer to use Jim as a surrogate. The boy is certainly not an everyman or even the universal lonely boy that Elliott was in *E.T.* But there is one motif that does have the blockbuster element of visceral identification: the often-noted airplane scenes. Spielberg's visual imagination "soars" with these scenes. He photographs the ceremony of the kamikaze pilots against the sun from Jim's admiring point of view. The tour de force comes with the American attack on the Japanese airfield across the fence from the labor camp. The camera pans with Jim as he climbs up to watch the attacking planes. He even receives a salute

Jim is on the same level as the attacking P-51 Mustang in Empire.

from a P-51 Mustang pilot who is flying in at the boy's eye level. Spielberg plunges us into Jim's crazed worship of the destruction from above, but he does not put the camera in the attacking planes. They are mysterious to us, we do not see them even as they airdrop supplies to the starving survivors of the war. It is a visual expression of the contemporary relationship of America to the world, where America is a distant lofty power with little ground-based knowledge of other peoples.

The filmmaker's ambition for his craft was too big to considerably scale down the budget for small boutique audiences. He had spent a lot of money for the real thing. The production team went through the costly procedures that it took to become the first American movie company to shoot in mainland China. They used the actual locations of Shanghai to good effect before moving on to complete the film in Spain.

The resulting negative costs were too large for the audience that was interested, particularly when only the foreign audience supported *Empire*. In 1987 the interest of the foreign audience (dominated by Europeans) showed an increasing divergence of taste and sensibility between Europe and the increasingly complacently self-isolated America.

John Boorman's *Hope and Glory* (1987) was a comparable film about a boy living in London during the blitz. The situation was less extreme and the ambitions of the movie were less poetic. The budget was lower and therefore it was viewed as a greater success, although its audience was smaller. *Hope and Glory* was co-produced by Goldcrest, the company that had created a market for historical films. But Goldcrest had fallen on hard times as its budgets increased to try to match the general inflation of major motion picture productions. The company would soon stop active production and only engaged in limited distribution. Bernardo Bertolucci's *The Last Emperor* (1987), an epic set in twentieth-century China, did better than *Empire* in the domestic market. This must have also been a sore spot for Spielberg.

Spielberg had made a breakthrough but as had been typical for him, his relative lack of audience caused him to readjust. His next three films were *Indiana Jones and The Last Crusade*, *Always*, and *Hook*. Both McBride and Freer lump these three together as a retreat after the experiments of *The Color Purple* and *Empire*. Certainly Spielberg was not about to become a boutique filmmaker. He was swinging back into the mainstream, and yet not the same mainstream as it had existed prior to *The Color Purple*. Before 1986, Indiana Jones was an increasingly nihilistic all-American hero. *Close Encounters* and *E.T.* took the point of view of white suburban everypeople, and the ethics of these films were based on individual wish fulfillment. Now Spielberg was moving towards a different relationship with the audience.

We can see this clearly when he returns to the action genre with *The Last Crusade*. It was a blockbuster different from the other action films coming out at the time, and in stark contrast with Hollywood's American bravado. His turn towards presenting American stories in a world context had become permanent, despite the modest box office of *Empire*. It is not an overt conversion to political filmmaking. It is a loosening of style as Spielberg learns to court a global audience even before the Iron Curtain falls and Asia becomes more integrated with the American economy. He still immerses the audience in the action, but viewers are less certain what the right action is. This difference can be most easily understood in the emerging contrast between Spielberg and his colleagues in action/thriller filmmaking, which is discussed in the next chapter.

5

LOOKING TO THE PAST

While Spielberg was stumbling through a maturing process with *The Color Purple* and *Empire of the Sun*, the right-wing turn in Hollywood was hardening. . . .
. . . Literally.

"Hard-bodied" heroes ranging from Sylvester Stallone to Arnold Schwarzenegger dominated the action genre, which in turn dominated the blockbuster productions of the later part of the decade.

THE RISE OF THE HARD BODY

The 1985 release of *Rambo: First Blood Part II* inspired several blockbuster movies to embrace the nihilism of right-wing reaction. Already in *First Blood Part I* (1982) the character of John T. Rambo (Sylvester Stallone) had elements of the emerging hard-body ethic. Susan Jeffords has identified this ethic as a movie representation of the Reaganite anti-government ideology. She identifies other important landmarks in this budding sub-genre, in particular *Lethal Weapon* (1987) and *Die Hard* (1988). While there were many, many more, these three were the biggest tent poles for their studios. All three movies initially spawned at least two sequels apiece. *Lethal Weapon* went to a fourth installment eleven years after its first. Surprisingly enough, there has been another cycle of sequels from these series twenty or more years after they were first made. Even so late in the day they proved their financial clout.

In contrast to *Raiders*, which embraced antecedents from 1940s Saturday-matinee specials, the hard-body films had a more immediate origin in the vigilante movies of the 1970s. Before the weakening and final demise of the Production Code in the period of 1966 to 1968, such nihilism was prohibited. Following the demise, vigilante titles such as *Dirty Harry* (1971) and *Death Wish* (1974)[18] blatantly showed middle-class America falling apart due to the depredations of violent savages, their subsequent coddling by liberals, and the sheer incompetence of government in responding to either the criminals or the liberals. There had been an expansion of legal rights in the 1960s and a concurrent wave of urban riots that swept the United States. The stories were obvious responses that flattered the conservative belief that the expansion of rights was linked to a breakdown of order. The movie series did try to soften an implied racism by casting white villains and even African American allies of the good guys. But such isolated castings against racial stereotypes did not relieve their portrayals of American cities as nonwhite hellish zones. Critics labeled these films as politically reactionary and the audience embraced them as such.

An earlier Hollywood that conformed to a production code had rarely dared to portray the law as an obstacle to safety. *Dirty Harry* and the other vigilante films were quite willing to step over that line. The legal obstacles to justice

were not just a matter of an isolated corrupt cop or a mis-
guided judge. Injustice was now represented as inherent in
the very mechanisms of legal procedure itself. Moviemakers
were not timid about their portrayals of an ineffective
government. It was somewhat shocking to see mainstream
Hollywood films condemn the system from a right-wing
point of view but there was a profitable audience for such
condemnations.

Yet even in the 1970s, story logic dictated that there was
a price to pay for vigilante action. In *Dirty Harry* and *Death
Wish* the heroes were isolated and did their good deeds in
defiance of their society. In return, they never got the thanks
of the society they tried to protect. Their task was mostly
unappreciated and they continued to be alone. It was not
until their sequels started being produced in the 1980s that
the characters were acknowledged as heroes by their fellow
citizens. This new appreciation came as the election of Reagan
amplified the anti-government tone even further. Vigilantes
now received the thanks of a grateful public, a public that
believed fervently that the law did not provide enough pro-
tection without necessary help from the illegal actions of
the hero.

The Rambo series was the story line that provided this
transition. The first movie (*First Blood Part I*) showed the
absolute isolation of the Vietnam veteran who has been
trained to survive and to kill. After provocation he killed a
sheriff's deputy in order to survive, and his lawlessness was
only slightly redeemed when he surrendered to the law at the
end of the movie. At the beginning of the second movie
(*Rambo: First Blood Part II*) John T. Rambo is serving hard
time for his destructions in the first movie. He is released,
however, in order to do something that the government will
not do: rescue American prisoners of war still held by the
Vietnamese. But the US government is not sincere about

John T. Rambo (Sylvester Stallone) was the ur-hard body.

supporting the mission and Rambo has to physically attack an American official who has betrayed him. It is significant that after this attack, Rambo is not punished. By the third installment Rambo is fulfilling both social and governmental expectations by fighting the Soviets in Afghanistan. The Rambo transition from scorned outlaw to official hero is confirmed by the Lethal Weapon series, which celebrates the violent behavior of Sergeant Martin Riggs. This series firmly establishes the bonding of white and black policemen who together break the law in the pursuit of justice. *Die Hard* also adopts this strategy and goes further in letting the onscreen public celebrate the violent tactics of John McClane.

Jeffords writes, "In contrast [to the 70s] the heroes of hard body films suggest a different kind of social order, one in which the men who are thrust forward into heroism are not heroic in defiance of their society but in defiance of their government and institutional bureaucracies" (19). These action movies became a cultural expression for male anxiety as the workplace (including the military) let more women into a variety of jobs. Right-wing action filmmakers more openly questioned the new public role of women in their own films. *Die Hard*'s McClane has a hard time adjusting to his wife's career, and there is a suggestion that she is willing to rebalance the marriage as a reward for his heroism.

Fred Pfeil also links these films to the law-as-obstacle politics of the United States.

> *In [Lethal Weapon 2's] final confrontation, Rog [good cop], having taken the cue, will complete the sentence that Arjen Rudd [bad guy], having just gunned down Riggs [other good cop], has begun—'Diplomatic immunity'—with 'has just been revoked,' with a bullet of his own. In the same way, . . . in Die Hard . . . an exchange . . . [between] . . . McClane [good cop] and the first of Gruber's gang that he kills (Bad Guy: 'You won't hurt me 'cause you're a policeman; there are rules for policemen.'/McClane (as he starts the fight that ends in his opponent's death); 'Yeah? That's what my captain keeps telling me.'). Through such rhymes and echoes still another link in the slippery chain linking Brothers to Others is forged in the form of a tacit agreement between heroes and villains that state and legal institutions finally have nothing to do with is really going on. (Pfeil, 167–68)*

Alan Nadel also emphasizes that by the end of the Reagan administration, heroic illegality had spread to the fact-based fictions of *Mississippi Burning* (1988) and *The Untouchables* (1987). Both these films are "about young idealistic law enforcers who, coaxed by veteran subordinates, realize that in order to combat criminals they have to embrace lawlessness" (Nadel, 1997, 132). While there are many films in Hollywood's vaults that portrayed the hero outside the law, this cycle was unique in insisting that there are no consequences to such illegality.

SPIELBERG REJECTS THE HARD BODY

Shortly after the 1984 release of *Temple of Doom*, Spielberg had this to say about the second Rambo movie; "I love *Rambo*. But I think it is potentially a very dangerous movie, because it's a this-is-the-way-it-should-have-been motion picture . . . It changes history in a frightening way . . . Even a bleeding heart liberal walks out trying desperately to deny they were entertained" (Breskin, 72). He was anticipating that his own audience did not want the mythic compensation of a hard body.

The late 1980s evolution of the action genre inspired Spielberg to put distance between the Indiana Jones character and white male dominance. He rejected scripts that might open up the film to charges of racism (McBride, 400–401). He denied himself the opportunity for the egregious colonialism of the previous two Raider movies by safely confining most of the story's action to Europe and the United States. The violence is mostly white on white. Indiana Jones even meets the ultimate Aryan: Adolf Hitler. The only exception is an exotic cult of Levantine protectors of the Grail but Indy eventually treats them as allies. The filmmaker also portrayed a capable female character who outwits Jones at several turns. Lucas, Spielberg, Zemeckis, Landis, and their cohort had been notorious for superficial treatment of female characters.[19] But in *Last Crusade*, Spielberg and Lucas introduced a female antagonist who was a match for the protagonist. Initially the audience may have interpreted Dr. Elsa Schneider (Alison Doody) as another sidekick whose ability to affect the action would fade, like Willie Scott and Marion Ravenswood in the previous films. But she was revealed to be a double-dealing Nazi agent whose powers remain potent until her final defeat. It seemed that the team was finally ready to write in a sexual and formidable woman as a contrast to the standard juvenile treatment of women in the 1940s Saturday-matinee genre.

The Last Crusade has hardly any references to American exceptionalism, which is also in contrast to its contemporary action films. The main action is far from the United States, although the movie's prologue is set in an iconic American West (a rather forced homage to John Ford). Indeed Harrison Ford seems to be the only American actor among the good guys. He contrasts with the decidedly non-American tweediness of his father Henry Jones (Sean Connery), colleague Dr. Marcus Brody (Denholm Elliot), and sidekick Sallah (John Rhys-Davis). The non-American aspect was mirrored in the box office. It grossed a hundred million more dollars overseas than it did here ($197m domestic, $297m foreign). This is a ratio of 40/60, which was approximately the same for *Empire* but at the considerably higher level of $495 million gross worldwide. This becomes the first time that a major Spielberg movie did so much better overseas even while doing a smash box office business here in the United States. The Spielberg earning power had not diminished while he had gone off on his "serious" tangent, and now that he had returned to the action game, he did not have to play by the hard-body rules. Indeed his soft-body action hero helped him reach the number two spot in the US box office for 1989.

THE COMPETITION IN HOLLYWOOD

Paramount cleverly got *The Last Crusade* into the theaters a month before the Warner Brothers colossus *Batman* opened. The Warner film was decidedly more disturbing than any of the Indiana Jones movies. Its story was set in a Gotham City that was falling apart; order could only be maintained by a vigilante. Tom Shone quotes Jon Peters, a high-powered

Batman producer, applauding the project as "a great opportunity to have this guy kick some ass" (189). Although the director Tim Burton sometimes resisted this hyper-violence, Shone accurately summarizes *Batman* as *"Death Wish* in a batsuit." The vigilante Batman was actually sought out by the hapless police for assistance. Thus it was fully in the spirit of American reactionary politics and became the top moneymaker for the year. It did not do as well overseas, reversing the *Last Crusade* split to 60/40 ($252m domestic, $161m foreign [IMDB]). Overseas it did barely half the business that *The Last Crusade* did. Several European countries severely restricted young people's access to the movie, hurting earnings disproportionately since they constituted the primary audience. The ratio suggests that Spielberg, in contrast to his rivals, was moving more adroitly to build a global audience and to become the US's biggest filmed entertainment export.

Nonetheless, *Batman* was the more influential model than *Last Crusade* for many studios, since it was the prototype for cross-media marketing. The late 1980s was a time when Hollywood studios underwent a further integration into transnational media conglomerates. Ancillary markets such as global television and video now returned more revenue than the traditional American box office. The blockbuster system was now maturing across various media.

Batman originated as a comic book title owned by DC Comics. DC was owned by Warner, which also had a major record division handling Prince, the featured songwriter for the movie *Batman*. Warner, of course, had further divisions that handled the foreign and ancillary market sales of *Batman* and the merchandising of action figures and other retail items. The movie was the engine for the revitalization of the Batman franchise, which delivered a multi-source, multi-decade revenue stream for the company. Warner Communications released it as it was merging with Time-Life. The

Time-Warner merger gave further impetus to cross-media marketing since Time owned HBO and a strong cable franchise. It had a venerable print division that would often use the opportunity to promote Warner Bros. movies. Its magazines would generally promote entertainment and movies as the center of that world. An anecdote illustrates the corrupting logic of these new "synergies." The first editor of *Entertainment Weekly* (a Time Warner magazine) was scolded in 1990, not for allowing negative reviews of Warner movies, but for allowing too many negative reviews of movies in general (Jarvis).

The hyper-marketing of films matched the hyper-marketing of the general culture. Oligopolies emerged in many industries in addition to film and there was little discussion of these developments that would have alarmed reformers of previous eras. Citizens seemed distracted by the market and their political awareness was limited. Americans were eager to ignore the aggressive actions that their government took, ostensibly on their behalf.[20] Even the end of the Cold War in 1989/1990 got only a lackluster response in popular culture. There were no Hollywood scripts on either perestroika (economic decentralization) or glasnost (democratization). Just as Americans showed little interest in their Cold War victory they were relatively passive over China's brutal suppression of the Tiananmen Square democracy movement. The end of communism was not a moment for reflection; it was just an opportunity for more market capitalism.

Spielberg mirrored this lack of engagement with current events when he remade an old Hollywood sentimental wartime romance—*A Guy Named Joe* (1944)—into *Always*. It was released in December of 1989. The wartime story was made for an audience that itself was making a collective sacrifice to win the war. Critics complained the updating of an already contrived fairy tale robbed the story of its one redeeming quality: that it honored sacrifice. The story itself had little to say in 1989, when no one was sacrificing for the greater good. There was no reason to assume that it would find an audience and it did not.

In January 1991, Spielberg committed to *Hook*, another contemporary treatment of an earlier fiction. In this case it was the turn of the previous century's play *Peter Pan*. Here the update conceit was that Peter had grown up to become a Wall Street buccaneer. Spielberg and his writers twisted and turned as to where to go from there. They could not bring themselves to condemn or to celebrate Peter's careerism. Instead they, like Peter's own petulant children, could only whine that Peter did not have the ability to spend more quality time with his family. The film reduced the imaginative phase of childhood to a mere obsession with magic and wish fulfillment.

The movie covered its bets by staging a spectacular version of Never-Neverland and using such charismatic hams as Robin Williams and Dustin Hoffman. It came in with an estimated negative cost of $70 million. This was twice what Spielberg had ever spent before and almost three times the average budget for a major film in 1991. The expensive sets were adequate compensation for the audience, who came out to give the film a very good if not great box office. They knew that the film would deliver the pleasures of Peter Pan. The Spielberg brand name worked wonders overseas where the box office was one-third greater than in the domestic market.

Henry Sheehan was one critic who championed Spielberg's treatment of maturity in *Hook*. On the other side, McBride more convincingly argued that Spielberg the artist was observed to be detached and bored by this project. Already the fantasy genre was being overtaken by a string of highly successful full-length animations coming out from Disney. In 1991, *Hook* had to divide the audience with *Beauty and the Beast.* In 1992, *Aladdin* topped the domestic box office, recapturing Walt Disney's financial success with full-length animation, if not his artistry. In this context *Hook* was Spielberg's last foray into the family genre per se. The audiences that Lucas and Spielberg had happily combined were now splitting apart into action/adventure and full-length animation.

THE YEAR 1993

By 1993 the breakup of communism was not going as peacefully as it had done in 1990. Yugoslavia was being torn apart by ethnic nationalism. The specter of genocide was again present on the European continent. The United States, having effortlessly ousted Iraq from Kuwait in 1991, ignored the Balkan troubles. But Spielberg was inspired by dark European headlines to look again at the scripts based on Thomas Kenneally's *Schindler's Ark.* The project about a German protector of Jews during the Holocaust was now called *Schindler's List.* Over the years the filmmaker had vacillated on this project, but this time he was ready. At the same time, he expressed interest in a dinosaur movie. Universal had bought the movie rights to Michael Crichton's 1990 bestseller *Jurassic Park.* It was a combination of circumstances that intertwined the two projects. Crichton had urged Spielberg to direct *Jurassic Park.* Meanwhile Spielberg was insistent on *Schindler's List* even though he was telling people that it would lose money. Nonetheless, Sid Sheinberg, representing Universal, the owner of both properties, used Spielberg's pessimism to pressure him to do *Jurassic Park* first. Spielberg ended up doing the two films back-to-back.

The year 1993 became an *anno mirabilis* for Steven Spielberg. *Jurassic Park* returned him to the top as the maker of the biggest moneymakers, while *Schindler's List* finally established his artistic worth (with the external validation of a Best Director Oscar). Both were global event films that attracted larger audiences overseas than in the United States. In other ways, the two films could not be more different. While Spielberg was increasingly referring to a split between his serious films and his popcorn movies, it is nonetheless the same man who made both sets of films. Both sets represent a continuous ambition to show the power of the filmic imagination. Both 1993 films engaged problems of representing what once existed, and now exists no longer. The director set out to validate audiences' faith in the power of the photorealistic story. Of course the narrative stakes are radically different in a story of the Holocaust from those in the tale of marauding T-Rexes.

In *Jurassic Park* a problem becomes apparent that had been dormant since *Duel*. In the earlier film Spielberg demonstrated that he could give the audience a riveting experience with exciting uses of the camera. Part of the excitement was the realism of the photographic image. The logic and status of film imagery comes from its photographic relationship with the world, which is so direct and immediate that viewers typically think it is more objectively powerful than either painting or literature. The American philosopher Charles Peirce called this an indexical relationship, and contrasted it with a merely conventional relationship (symbolic) or a resemblance relationship (iconic), which are the relations literature and painting have with the represented world. Of course the indexical image cannot be a truly objective reflection of an exterior reality. There is always a subjective mind creating the image. Nonetheless, viewers have always given film imagery a high level of credibility because of this indexical relationship. Film theorists ranging from Siegfried Krakauer to Andre Bazin have spoken of the superior potential of film as an art precisely because of this indexical status.

They value the camera's ability to reveal a material world that exceeds the filmmaker's imagination. Now computer imagery has challenged their assumptions.

During pre-production, Spielberg was contemplating the use of models, as provided by Stan Winston on previous movies. He knew that he could enhance the models by using computer imaging, and so he auditioned a film that created representations of dinosaurs using only the digital-image software. The computer programs could now handle the intricate detail of skin texture, and could model constantly changing shadows. The computers exceeded the limits of an individual's imagination. No one person could anticipate the shadows and shifting skin textures of an animal's movement, but the accumulation of various software applications could do this on an efficient basis. The producers were amazed at the program's realism and decided that the image of a moving dinosaur was able to match photographic standards. This raised a new aesthetic challenge for the filmmaker.

By 1993, then, computers could mimic the photographic camera. In digital imagery, nothing has to be placed in front of a camera and recorded. The entire image can be created inside the computer and then told to move according to algorithms that have been designed by computer software writers. There is no indexical relationship with a represented world, only the one of resemblance—as in painting. This is not much of a problem for viewers, who are generally willing to suspend their skepticism about the reality of an image in order to believe in the story. It is a problem for the filmmakers. There is first the logistical problem of creating images that combine photorealism and digital resemblance. Real-world actors had to act against blue screens with imagined digital animals to be added later. The more profound problem is for the filmmaker who can no longer rely on the materiality of the represented world to compensate for the limits of his or her own imagination. *Jurassic Park* now precipitated a crisis that had been quietly brewing since the early uses of computer-aided imagery in *2001: A Space Odyssey* (1968) and *Star Wars* (1977).

Spielberg was going to use digital dinosaurs, but how was he going to make sure of the audience reaction? Would they still get excited even when they watched dinosaurs that had obviously not been captured in the actual world but simulated in the computer? Would the audience merely accept the dinosaurs as they accepted the animated people and creatures of *Aladdin* (1992)? Or worse yet, would they treat the dinosaur with no more respect than the accepted wonders of actual trained animals in such films as *Free Willy* (1993)? In other words, would the dinosaurs be no big deal? Would they not be awed by the digital dinosaurs fully integrated into the photorealistic world?

Spielberg could not leave the audience's reaction to chance. He designed the film to guide audience responses through the surrogates of the paleontologists Grant (Sam Neill) and Sattler (Laura Dern), particularly through a prolonged reaction sequence when they first encounter the digital dinosaurs. The sequence begins as the jeeps pull up to a stop in a meadow on Jurassic Island. In the first jeep, Grant first reacts to something we cannot see. Then he directs his fellow passenger, Sattler, to take a look at what we cannot see, radically delaying our own pleasure until the master shot, which combines both the paleontologists and the towering Brachiosaurus in one shot. Of course it had to be a master shot that showed both, and not their point-of-view shot, since the cinematic payoff is not only that Spielberg can create a dinosaur but that he can also convincingly combine the dinosaur with the photographic elements, i.e., the human actors, within the same space.

A virtuoso matching of photorealism and digital imagery. The great reveal of the Brachiosaurus with tiny humans in the foreground in Jurassic Park.

This hyper-manipulation was overdetermined. Within the movie it made sure that the audience would respond to the spectacle of the movie as something truly pioneering, which the digital imagery actually was. Outside the movie, the spectacle also drove the marketing and merchandising of the film. Many filmic choices were made in order that the movie create a perfect marketing experience, and foremost among those choices was the virtual reality of the movie. Once the dinosaurs start attacking they are fast and furious and are directed at the camera as much as at the on-screen prey. The frontal assaults were scary enough to earn a PG-13 from a very tolerant ratings board. The production team had made the decision to forego the youngest potential members of the audience in order to enhance the impact on the rest of the audience.

Did the hyper-reality of the dinosaurs cause the audience to grow skeptical about filmic realism? Perhaps the skepticism was due to the extra-textuality of the very intense marketing. "By the time it opened, I was so bored by the hype I really didn't care if I saw it or not. I finally did see it . . . and was not really impressed . . . Spielberg's heart really wasn't in it." This quote was a typical remark from one part of the audience (Stempel, 164). Many were put off by the extraordinary publicity machine. It was probably not just a matter of too much marketing, but an erosion of the film's status. The film itself was conceived in anticipation of the marketing, as was *Batman* four years previous. Timothy Corrigan has used the felicitous phrase that blockbusters have become "advertisements for themselves" and certainly no film fits that more than *Jurassic Park*. Within a year the one billion dollars in merchandising revenue exceeded the $900 million in worldwide ticket sales (Busch).

Jurassic Park was both an unprecedented marketing effort and a new standard for computer-generated imagery (CGI). CGI and the marketing resonated with each other and suggested that there was an underlying cause common to both. The dual aspects did inspire the debate that has gone on since about whether the spectacularity of the digital image subverts the narrative function of movies. It is an argument that started when Lucas and Spielberg had launched their blockbusters in the 1970s before the computer revolution really started. In hindsight their vision of movies motivated the development of CGI.[21] Their emphasis on immersive experience was and is part of the same structure of feeling as the subsequent development of virtual reality technologies. What was now new to the movies was that computer images allowed a complete freedom from the actual. Previously the limitation of the photographic camera was itself a useful discipline on the director's vision of how to represent the world.

Digital manipulation started to acquire political connotations since it was being closely linked, through movies such as *Terminator 2* (1993), to nihilistic visions of the apocalypse. These visions often served as backdrops for the actions of hard-bodied heroes engaged in saving the world from annihilation. The portrayal of these threats made fearful thinking more natural for the audience and became an increasing part of the political dialogue in the years leading up to 2001. Before the extraordinary power of digital enhancement, photorealism was a more appropriate aesthetic for more realistic views of threats. Thus the old-fashioned traditional way of making films tended towards a less threatened view of the world and a more nuanced view of how to resolve conflict.

In typical Spielberg ambiguity, *Jurassic Park* had both existential threats (the unrelenting attacks of the carnivorous dinosaurs) and a benign view of the world (the survivors escape while the dinosaurs remain confined to an island). The heroes of *Jurassic Park* included the female paleontologist and absolutely no vigilantes or hard bodies. As Hollywood turned to more apocalyptic films using the techniques pioneered in *Jurassic Park*, Spielberg responded. His sequel to *Jurassic Park*, *Lost World* (1997), tended towards the apocalypse and his 2005 *War of the Worlds* even appropriated the hard-body ethos to feature a hero engaged in extralegal violence. Digital imagery tied Spielberg to the extreme genre of fear and paranoia that I will discuss below.

RETURN TO PHOTOREALISM: *SCHINDLER'S LIST*

But he was also pursuing historical realism at the same time, and his techniques were evolving rapidly. In this genre the match between the actual world and the representation poses a strong moral problem. Is classic fictional photorealism adequate to the great tragedy of Western civilization? *Schindler's List* has elements of experiential filmmaking, and of immersing the audience without asking them to reflect. A movie about Oskar Schindler is already an act of fictional reduction. The Hollywood team reduces the story further by writing a script simple enough to fit the definition of high concept. It is of a dissolute German making the righteous decision to save Jews during World War Two. Will photorealism restore a dimensionality lacking in the script?

The Nazis decide to destroy the Jewish ghetto in Krakow at the same time that a civilian Nazi, Oskar Schindler (Liam Neeson), sets up a small factory using Jewish labor and the skills of the local Jewish businessmen, primarily Itzhak Stern (Ben Kingsley). As the military commander Amon Goeth (Ralph Fiennes) continues to kill and to abuse the displaced Krakow Jews, now living in a camp in Plaszow, Schindler allows his factory to be used as a refuge for those Jews who are placed on the list to work there. Schindler, at first, simply seems to be an opportunist, but he takes increasingly proactive steps to save his Jewish workers as the authorities ship people off to the death camp at Auschwitz. As long as he keeps bribing the military officers he is effective. In the final moments of the war Schindler uses his entire fortune to buy the safety of 1,100 Jews from Goeth. The story ends as the 1,100 meet a soldier from the advancing Red Army. Schindler flees the Russians, while Goeth is executed. The film has an epilogue of the real surviving Jews, escorted by the film's actors, placing stones of remembrance on the Israeli grave of the real Oskar Schindler.

There had been a handful of American films about the genocides of World War Two, but it was the TV mini-series *Holocaust* (NBC, April 16–19, 1978) that had been the most prominent previous entry into the politics of popular memory.

The TV show riveted American audiences and is considered responsible for the German nation finally using the word "holocaust" (IMDB site). Although *Holocaust* uses completely fictional characters while *Schindler's List* uses fictionalized historical figures, it could be argued that the television mini-series, which lasted more than eight hours, had a larger historical vision. The TV show had memorable sketches of working-class Jews and depicted the different politics of the Jewish world at the time, including communists. It showed the various levels of commitment of the Nazis, ranging from true believers to opportunists. In contrast, Spielberg represents communities without ideology—not fascism; not even anti-fascism. In the film, the cataclysm proceeds as a force of nature and the only political question is what to do to survive the storm.

Nonetheless *Schindler's List* has the forceful impact of a major motion picture and continues to shape our historical memory. Its force comes from its status as a film made by a film artist. The TV show *Holocaust* suffers from a typical "small screen" television style, with neither the camera work nor the editing surprising or challenging the audience. *Schindler's List* is a constant negotiation between a tentative "objective" image that shocks us and subjective realisms that cater, indeed pander, to our collective memory of the tragedy. With this in mind we should take with a grain of salt the claim that Spielberg finally gave up his famous obsession with pleasing the audience. "I've always cared about everybody liking the movie . . . and this was the one film, the one subject that I didn't care who liked it or didn't like it" (Hollywood Foreign Press Association, Dec. 9, 1993, p. 3).

Typically, the director was adamant about shooting in Poland and although he was prevented from shooting on the actual Auschwitz location, he constructed an "authentic" set as close to the actual site as possible. The Polish shoot was uncomfortable for many cast and crew members, because of the memories buried in the landscape and some unrepentant local people, but Spielberg's aesthetic ambitions made it necessary. He chose to use black-and-white photography printed onto color stock.[22] Of course black-and-white is not true to the actual events, only to our memory of the coverage of those events. His photography addresses our experience of actual footage from the war and of 1940s Hollywood movies, reassuring us that our experience is accurate, is real.

Language is also treated with the same logic. Spielberg follows the old filmic convention of using the language of the audience rather than the language of the actual characters. This convention has been challenged several times in the 1980s, particularly in Westerns, but is still dominant. The convention dictates that the entire film is in English, and for the most part it is. However, Spielberg allows bits and pieces of Hebrew, Yiddish, and German as it suits his dramatic purposes: Hebrew for religious rituals, Yiddish for secret talk, German for harsh commands.

Thrill-ride immersion operates at the level of the camera work. Spielberg is torn between keeping the audience distant from the horrible events and immersing us within the story. This tension explains the controversial scene where the women are sent to the showers in Auschwitz. The camera is in among them, capturing their anguish over the rumors they have heard about the showers actually being gas chambers. The viewers as well as the women have every right to believe this is the end as they are herded into the shower room and the door is locked. To immerse the audience even further in the women's primal experience, the lights go out on screen, which naturally throws the audience into darkness as well. But then water comes out of the shower heads and the diegetic lights come up, drawing a sigh of relief from the on-screen women and, one hopes, from the theater audience as well.

Spielberg has taken us to the brink but has not let either the characters or the viewers go over it.

As in the case of *E.T.*, Spielberg announced that he did not storyboard *Schindler's List*. Instead, he staged the entire action, and used several cameras to capture it. Take for instance some of chaotic moments during the liquidation of the ghetto, when German soldiers are shooting uncooperative Jews dead without warning. Some people know the script (the actor knows he or she is to be killed, as does the soldier who must fire the blank in the gun at the victim). Other actors do not know the exact course of action. Ben Kingsley reported that in such a situation the acting comes more from primordial conditioning than from training and skill. He recalled running in shock when the woman next to him fell down (Hollywood Foreign Press Association, Dec. 10, 1993). This was an immersion of the actor in the action, and it translated into an immersion of the audience, particularly when the camera was not framing or anticipating such improvised responses. The cameras in such scenes were constantly picking up little bits of shootings and other horrors at the edges of the frame, or moving in a pell-mell fashion to catch such action on the fly. The lack of framed and focused presentation of horror denied the audience the chance to examine it. Instead they felt impulses to respond physically, triggered by the peripheral awareness of these events on the edge.

The film was released November 30, 1993, and earned a worldwide box office gross of $317 million. The reporters and critics of the media world were unstinting in their admiration of the director's transition from entertainer to artist. Within four months the movie won the Academy Award for Best Picture and Spielberg got his first Oscar for directing. He may have noticed that he actually experienced another breakthrough (albeit a minor one) by attracting sustained academic interest. *Schindler's List* is the most debated

Spielberg movie in intellectual circles. The debate involved the appropriateness of a fiction movie's strategies to the tragedy of the twentieth century. Claude Lanzmann denounced *Schindler's List* and contrasted it with his own French documentary *Shoah* (1985), consisting of actual testimony from witnesses to the events. For Lanzmann, no fictional representation could be sufficient to describe the events, particularly the various Hollywood tricks of *Schindler's List*. Such a criticism not so subtly linked the movie to the manipulations of *Jurassic Park*.

These critics seem to regret that a Hollywood historical film cannot be made as a documentary. The historical actuality of the story suggests that it should be measured against the "objective" truth of history. While critical minds accept that such truth cannot be established even for a work of scholarship, the world of popular culture still wants the "truth" in a movie and debates whether it has been achieved. *Schindler's List* was the first time Spielberg subjected himself to such judgment in relation to the truth criterion. None of his previous blockbusters raised this issue. But the way of reaching such a "truth" is ironic; it is part of Hollywood's ethos that the audience is the ultimate arbiter of all questions of authenticity. Therefore the filmmaker's desire for acceptable "truth" often leads the historical filmmaker, who has this ethos, to adopt a consensual view of history that flatters audience assumptions about the past.

Both Spielberg and his audience believe strongly in the discursive power of fictional film. So deep is this belief that the filmmaker claimed the film was a response to the present. Spielberg told the press that an immediate impetus to finally make the movie was the desire to respond to the ethnic killing in Bosnia (Hollywood Foreign Press Association, Dec. 9, 1993, 2). He also went on to position his film as a response to the rise of neo-Nazis after the 1989 fall of the Berlin Wall.

These were political reasons. In addition he gave many aesthetic reasons, such as that he was finally ready and that a script had finally taken shape. There were external reasons such as the passing of the generation that had suffered through the genocide and the fading of memories of the war. Spielberg and his Hollywood brethren really believed that *Schindler's List* was a necessary validation of what was otherwise a fast-departing memory. Hansen points out that the Shoah left no surviving communities or even burial sites; "the remembrance of the Shoah, to the extent that it was public and collective, has always been dependent on mass-mediated forms of memory" (213).

Many elements of the film were designed to compel audience approval. There were the immersions, the easy identification of good versus evil, and the absence of reflections on why this evil is taking place. It was neither surprising nor inappropriate that this film was made by the pioneer of the blockbuster. But as Hansen argued, this acknowledgment of the popular did not mean a critical dismissal of the film. It is a function of popular movie-making that it normalizes subject matter, and in this case the movie allows society to think again about the unbearable past. The movie becomes a consensual historical film.

Schindler's List was, however, a relatively easy look at the past. Spielberg immerses us in a terrible situation, but is careful not to numb or overwhelm our emotions. He does this by giving us safe zones, particularly around the presence of Schindler. It is telling that Oskar Schindler's original motivation is making money, and that through this self-centered concern, he is slowly led into the moral activity of saving people. Audiences embraced this story as a celebration of capitalism's inherent resistance to hatred and destruction. I argue, therefore, that although the movie asks us to share the sadness of the tragedies, it does not urge us to reform the present. It implies an acceptance of the present and the postwar success of Jews. Spielberg's engagement with history was emotional but did not challenge us to action. His use of history had not yet reached fulfillment.

HIATUS: TIME TO THINK

A four-year hiatus begins in 1994 for the filmmaker. Spielberg had passed yet another turning point in his career. He had burst upon the scene with *Jaws* and had reached superstardom with *E.T.* Now he was a full-fledged artist in the media discourse. His own artistic development had only begun, however. He had barely started exploring the filming of history. There was a lack of urgency around world politics and the domestic situation, as the wars in the Balkans wound down and President Clinton and the Congress settled down to a series of dysfunctional impasses. Prior to the release of *Jurassic Park* and *Schindler's List*, the American electorate finally restored a Democrat to the White House, because the Republican President George Bush was unresponsive to the 1991–1992 recession that Americans were suffering through. The election of Bill Clinton was not a repudiation of twelve years of Republican administrations, however. Clinton was a card-carrying member of the Democratic Leadership Council (DLC), which was formed in 1988 to get rid of the party's hostility to big business, and to put more distance between the Democratic Party and labor. This paralleled a European movement called "the third way," which entailed a lessening of government's promise to provide social welfare and an embrace by leftish political leaders of aspects of privatization. Clinton's election was not a pendulum swing away from the privatization policies of the Republicans. It was merely a less ideological version of pro-big business attitudes.

Bill Clinton was famous for his ability to woo an audience and to express a heartfelt empathy that people could feel personally. In this and in other matters he was the political equivalent of audience-loving Steven Spielberg, and Spielberg in time became a famous "friend of Bill." Spielberg's own contradictory combination of populist inclusiveness and faith in individualism was completely in tune with domestic American politics. Clinton was creating a White House that was sensitive to the politics of domestic multiculturalism and international cooperation in foreign affairs but did not have much regard for restoring the welfare network. Thus both the filmmaker and the president were finessing the union of sunbelt lack of concern about public welfare with liberal inclusionary rhetoric.

Globalization was both an opportunity and problem for both men. Spielberg was solidifying his international audience. *Schindler's List* was the first film he made without one American star in it. Of the $310 million box office, 70 percent came from overseas, which is the largest percentage he ever achieved from this source. Meanwhile, the $563 million foreign tickets sold for *Jurassic Park* was the largest absolute number for any American film. This occurred as governments were trying to negotiate a cultural exemption to free trade; *Jurassic Park* became the sign of a big Hollywood film destroying other national film industries. For example, the French government complained about *Jurassic Park* siphoning off the French audience for the local big-budget film *Germinal*. Spielberg was sensitive to such charges and avowed his love of all national cinemas even as he decried attempts to impose quotas on American films. The Clinton administration fought French efforts to impose quotas on Hollywood although ultimately the French were somewhat successful in their European-oriented television policy.

While Spielberg basked in his enhanced public status, receiving global acclaim for his filmmaking and making a friend in the White House, he formed a partnership with Jeffrey Katzenberg and David Geffen to create a new studio: DreamWorks SKG. This company eventually enjoyed success, but did not overcome the high entry barriers to new film studios. To overcome this, its film division has been merged with several old-line major studios since 2005. DreamWorks is an interesting company that may yet revive its independence (Barnes). During this entire period, Spielberg continued his own personal relationships with other studios. DreamWorks' existence, however, influenced the decisions that Spielberg made regarding which projects he would direct and when. DreamWorks was an engine for the historical epic revival productions. Spielberg's own *Amistad* (1997) and *Saving Private Ryan* (1998) joined the animated *Prince of Egypt* (1998) and Ridley Scott's *Gladiator* (2000) to reinvigorate the genre (see Russell). The next chapter will examine the new uses Spielberg was making of history after *Schindler's List*.

THE DEVELOPMENT OF HISTORICAL STYLE

The filmmaker's relationship with the audience has come a long way from *The Color Purple* to *Schindler's List*. Prior to *Purple* Spielberg's blockbusters accommodated the right-wing turn of American politics, even if it is debatable that these films were promoting such a turn. But in the mid-1980s Spielberg veered off in another direction, away from the hard bodies of John T. Rambo, Martin Riggs, and John McClane. He had fallen out of step with the Reagan/Bush ideology and instead was recycling older approaches to film. The audience did not always follow, but by the early 1990s he had regained mass attention. He explored the darkest topic, even though his films remained light and sweet to the audience. His audience had shifted and become more international. The shift was decisive; we shall see how the films veered between a consensual view of history that accommodated the right-wing turn and explorations of socio-political contradictions. The stakes were too high with big-budget filmmaking to ever depart too much from the consensus, but the coming years made Spielberg take more of a stand in his storytelling.

6

THE HISTORICAL FILM

Can a blockbuster film really do the work of historical imagination? The historical imagination is triggered by the problems of the present while typical blockbuster films dissolve
problems with decisive action and wish fulfillment. This is
the tension between social engagement and consensual myth-
making. Since 1993 Spielberg kept coming up against this
tension as he tried to create compelling strategies of realism.
It was obvious that he had been successful at reaching
consensus with *Schindler's List* and that various audiences
responded well. It was equally obvious that his next attempt
with *Amistad* (1997) was less successful, with only a few positive responses. Immediately after, Spielberg regained his
massive audience and global attention with the release of
Saving Private Ryan in 1998.

The realism strategies that Spielberg chose for his various
projects are fundamental to understanding his narrative
ambitions and the audience's response. Spielberg challenges
himself to present the audience with socio-political problems

while continuing to work in the blockbuster style. His peren-
nial desire to get the audience to like his films is a driving
motive behind a consensual approach. But as American
society becomes increasingly polarized in the new century,
and as the world starts to wonder about the basis of American
culture, there is another desire: to engage in social-problem
films. Spielberg takes on this additional motivation, and
balances the two impulses between films or, more subtly,
within the movies themselves. After *Schindler's List*, Spielberg's choice of projects often set up this tension in a
variety of engaged stories: *Amistad, Saving Private Ryan,
Minority Report, Munich*, and more. In his own mind he
also restores a balance by making *War of the Worlds* (2005)
and *Indiana Jones IV* (2008) as crowd pleasers. But even
with these supposed "popcorn" thrillers we see more engagement than the earlier romps of *Jaws* and *Raiders*. It seems
appropriate to investigate how his style has changed along
with the content.

CRITICAL FRAME: CONSENSUAL MYTHMAKING AND SOCIAL ENGAGEMENT

The film has a different relationship with society than the
novel. Millions of dollars are invested and a mass audience
must be attracted. Therefore the history that the film represents is a more overtly collective vision than the great novels.
It is no surprise that movies such as Laurence Olivier's *Henry
V* (1944) and Sergei Eisenstein's *Alexander Nevsky* (1938)
appeared during times of extreme national tensions. In such
times, the government, the film studios, and the audiences
form a consensus about the history, which the artist articu-
lates, casting consensual myth into the medium of film. The
US commercial film industry returned to social-problem

films after World War Two, starting with *The Best Years of Our Lives* in 1946. These films have a different relationship with society. They are not made with government collaboration or backing, nor do they even seek a broad ideological consensus, even though they attract a profitable audience who want to share the filmmakers' search. These films have the same ambition as a Sir Walter Scott, Honore Balzac or Leo Tolstoy novel, which is to describe the contradictions of society. The contradictions emerge in the story even if the storyteller does not have a clear understanding of these contradictions. This is because a story that is well narrated and not merely described will lead to a truthful representation of social contradictions, whether or not the storyteller consciously comprehends social complexity.

Big-budget filmmakers have a reluctance to engage in national or sectarian debates. Hollywood, due to the leadership of Spielberg and others, discovered how to excite the audience even while avoiding polarizing politics. The blockbuster must promise an unprecedented experience to a broad range of the global audience. This works against the passive realism of objective photography, and in favor of a visual pace that denies reflection. These considerations lead to a test for Spielberg's later films. Will his style of realism encourage or distract from reflection?

THE END OF THE HIATUS

Spielberg's pacing in *Schindler's List* had not been overly rapid. There was time for reflection. The director was telling such an overwrought story, however, that only one kind of reflection was morally acceptable. This film was made in the relative calm of the breakup of the Cold War and the global audience was ready for an American to make such an overdetermined film about the experiences of the Jewish genocide. After this the situation evolved and post-*Schindler* Spielberg was instinctive enough to turn to a more open-ended realism that could accommodate various responses.

Spielberg returned to directing by making the sequel, *Jurassic Park: Lost World* and a historical film, *Amistad*, back-to-back after a four-year hiatus. Both *Amistad* and *Lost World* were more extreme versions of *Schindler's List* and *Jurassic Park*. *Amistad* was extremely didactic and moralistic in its treatment of the past. *Lost World* sped up the action of *Jurassic Park* to showcase an even more convincing weaving together of computer images and photographic footage. Human character conflicts were initiated but soon fell by the wayside as the dinosaurs took over the movie. *Lost World* met expectations by earning more than two-thirds of what the original made while boosting the secondary market for Jurassic merchandise and theme park rides. *Amistad* performed poorly, with a disappointing box office of only $60 million globally. I estimate only 13 million people saw it.[23] While *Lost World* was just a corporate decision to make more money while having fun, however, *Amistad* was necessary for Spielberg to do in order to prepare himself for future engaged filmmaking. He needed to work out a sense of proportion between the various dichotomies of historical storytelling for subsequent projects.

AMISTAD AND A FAILURE AT MYTHMAKING

Spielberg was approached by the African American television actress and producer Debbie Allen to make a film about the actual events involving the slave ship *La Amistad* in 1839. His first phone call while contemplating the script was to an elder statesman of black actors, Morgan Freeman, who immediately endorsed the project and agreed to appear in it.

Spielberg's Word War Two project—*Saving Private Ryan*—
was already green-lighted to be filmed, but he postponed it.
He completed principal photography on *Amistad* in less than
two months.

The story begins when freshly captured African slaves
overwhelm the Spanish-Cuban crew on a ship in American
waters. They keep two Cubans alive to sail them back to
Africa. But the two men tack north by northeast rather than
directly east, and the ship is eventually seized by a US naval
ship off the coast of Long Island. Are the Africans free or are
they still property and thus part of the salvage of the ship?
The United States is headed towards civil war over slavery
and treatment of the Africans gets entangled in domestic
politics. The case goes all the way to the Supreme Court.
There the African case is argued by John Quincy Adams
(Anthony Hopkins), the former sixth US president and the
son of the second president. The Court sets the Africans free
and they return to Africa.

The film paralleled *Schindler's List*, with a cast of many
victims being saved by an outsider. But Allen and Spielberg
were determined to change the circumstances and to
empower the victims to a much greater extent than obtained
in the Holocaust story. There are both visual and musical
references to the earlier radical film *Burn* (1969) that strongly
emphasized the need for self-liberation against the trickery
of allowing others to bestow one's freedom upon one. The
movie begins with the drama of the slaves overpowering the
ship's crew on board *La Amistad*. A few days later, while *La
Amistad* is still under African control, it sails silently past an
American yacht full of upper-class couples dining on the
deck. They pause to look at the passing slaver, both ships
unable to comprehend or even interact with the other.
Other powerful and shocking images illustrate the testimony
of Cinque (Djimon Hounsou), who as the leader of the

Africans tells the court of the horrors of the slaver's middle passage. Nonetheless, *Amistad* is the least visual of Spielberg's work. The only shot that draws a visceral reaction is that of slaves being deliberately and brutally drowned at sea. There is little camera movement (Freer, 255). Instead of visual interest, the movie progresses in the linguistic sphere, to culminate not only in Adams' oration but also in Cinque's final remarks.

Unlike any other movie I have discussed so far, every word in this film is spoken in the correct historical language, be it Mende, Spanish, or English. This is an interesting strategy to establish a direct connection with the reality of the historical events. The issue of language accuracy is a plot point, since the primary problem for the white abolitionist advocates is to understand the Africans. Their first translator cannot really move beyond the rudiments and cannot really uncover the Africans' stories. Therefore the lawyer and his patrons search for someone who can translate adequately. They are successful in finding a bilingual African man, but they still struggle to understand the separate modes of thinking. Spielberg drops the usual Hollywood convention of assumed linguistic comprehension between allies.

This element gives the film a theme that was only touched on before in *Close Encounters, E.T.* and *Empire*; communication of intelligent beings across cultural divides. But in the previous films there were hints of magic or of some hidden facility for language. Here language is difficult; it is a real obstacle and the filmmaker looks directly at the hard reality of globalization. He gets away from assumptions of Eurocentricism in order to show that even Caucasians have to strain to learn the language of another race of people. In contrast, the erudite globe-trotting Indiana Jones is not shown learning, he already speaks Chinese and Indian dialects effortlessly in *Temple of Doom*.

The movie shows a greater sense of the power of historical filmmaking than Spielberg's previous efforts because it engages the current issue of whose story ought to be told. *Amistad* is a rebuke to Hollywood's previous major civil rights movie, *Mississippi Burning* (1988).[24] The earlier movie was told from a white person's point of view. The history of capturing the men responsible for the murder of three civil rights workers was distorted to make two white FBI agents into heroes who have to break the law in order to uphold it. Now in *Amistad* Spielberg emphasizes the majesty of the law and of telling one's story in court. He makes Adams and Cinque co-equals in articulating the story and even goes a step further. Adams finds common ground with Cinque in their mutual respect for their ancestors. Of course in Adams' case the ancestor is his own father, who was the second president of the United States. His appeal to the Supreme Court is based on family values. This is a deliberate misreading of the actual John Quincy Adams, who never met the actual Cinque, despite pleading the case. Adams's invocation of family values was a pure Spielberg concession to his generation's obsession with the intimacy of the family. Even a superficial reading of history reveals that the "passion to have a baby or spend more time with one's family was not high on the founders' list of public virtues" (Coontz, 97).

The filmmaker was bending history to fit his multicultural vision of a world where black Africans were political players as effective as white Euro-Americans. This was the wishful story that Spielberg wanted to tell Theo, his adopted African American son. In this case, his instinct to seek consensus with wish fulfillment works against the movie. Historians were not impressed with a deliberate falsification of the role of the abolitionist Lewis Tappen (Stellan Skarsgård) or the lawyer Roger Baldwin (Matthew McConaughey). The black freedman activist, Theodore Joadson (Morgan Freeman), became